GARDEN ENTERTAINING

GARDEN ENTERTAINING

From a Romantic Dinner for Two to an Arbor Wedding for Fifty...
The Complete Guide to Entertaining Outdoors

Text by Patricia Horan
Menus and Recipes by Hillary Davis
Garden Lists by Maria C. Gleason
Concept by Deirdre Colby and Maria C. Gleason

GROVE WEIDENFELD
NEW YORK

For my mother, with loving memories of your greenery at the
Boondocks, our magical garden in the summer sun.

A FRIEDMAN GROUP BOOK

Published in the United States by
Grove Weidenfeld
A Division of Grove Press, Inc.
841 Broadway
New York, New York 10003-4793

Library of Congress Cataloging-in-Publication Data
Horan, Patricia
Garden entertaining / Patricia Horan: menus and recipes by
Hillary S.S. Davis: plant lists by Maria C. Gleason:
concept by Deirdre Colby.—1st ed.
p. cm.
"A Friedman Group book."
ISBN 0-8021-1337-0 (alk. paper)
1. Landscape gardening. 2. Entertaining. 3. Gardens.
I. Davis, Hillary. II. Gleason, Maria C.
III. Colby, Deirdre. IV. Title.
SB473.H58 1991
712 .6—dc20 90-37892
CIP

GARDEN ENTERTAINING
was prepared and produced by
Michael Friedman Publishing Group, Inc.
15 West 26th Street
New York, New York 10010

Art Director: Jeff Batzli
Designer: Stephanie Bart-Horvath
Photo Researcher: Anne K. Price

Typeset by The Interface Group
Color Separations by Excel Graphic Arts Co.
Printed and bound in Hong Kong by LeeFung-Asco Printers Ltd.

First Edition 1991

10 9 8 7 6 5 4 3 2 1

CONTENTS

INTRODUCTION

A garden makes a delightful dining room. Divinely decorated, tirelessly making itself over, only a garden can surprise its guests with such marvels as the newly burst bulb or the exquisite hummingbird. Never did lovingly prepared food and drink enjoy a more felicitous setting. A party set up—lock, stock and Baccarat—out of doors where things are green and growing, is immediately enlivened and set free. Guests who would otherwise be sitting still are strolling, relaxed and enchanted. With our gardens we are creatures of the season, the mood, and the moment, and we like each other's company.

The days of the staid garden party are long gone. As the party-givers and goers interviewed on the following pages attest, garden entertaining, with its bugs and sudden cloudbursts, demands more thoughtful planning. But it also promises greater ease while the party is in progress. This is the opportunity to bend the rules, intentionally mismatch the china, and perhaps playfully improvise an amusing centerpiece out of something wonderful that blossomed while you were in the kitchen. When the air is breezy, so is the party.

Nothing comes to us as naturally as gathering in our gardens. There is proof of this through history, from Eden to Versailles and Winterthur. Images of the garden as paradise adorned Egyptian tomb paintings, Assyrian bas reliefs, Chinese scrolls, and illuminated manuscripts. The ancient Greeks constructed cool stone garden grottoes, watered by springs, in which to recline in hot weather and cultivated roof gardens in their cities. Roman villa gardens, too, were sybaritic, fanciful retreats, adorned with marble benches and dining tables as well as waterways in which wine jugs were suspended to cool and food floated to guests in dishes shaped like boats or birds.

In Renaissance times, hidden jets sprayed surprised guests in lively gardens. Further on down the path the same guests were serenaded by musical water fountains. A century before the West was to discover coffee, seventeenth-century Turkish garden party-goers held coffee klatches on ornate carpets while slaves sang and played. Chinese hosts challenged their guests to compose a poem before a cup of wine floated to the end of a winding channel. The guest who failed had to drink the entire cup of wine on the spot. A painting of a Sultan's garden party depicts living fruit trees, cypresses and tulips, as well as cages containing singing birds—and that is just what was on the cake.

The word "paradise" comes down to us from the Old Persian for "walled garden," and it is just that feeling of escape into another, better world that we seek to share with our friends. The seventeenth-century Japanese teahouse designers taught us the healing power of gardens by designing theirs specifically to aid visitors in shedding the cares of the world. Consciously or not, that is exactly what we try to do today when we entertain. A garden refuge, we have found, is a friend indeed. Perhaps that is what garden entertaining really is: the introduction of one dear friend to another.

Here, have a seat in the shade near the jasmine. Enjoy this cool drink while you listen for the whippoorwill. Relax and know you are in the best of all possible worlds.

"I envy you," wrote the Chinese poet Ch'ien Ch'i. "I envy you, drunk with flowers, butterflies swirling in your dreams."

© Derek Fell

PART I

GARDEN PLANNING AND PREPARATION

For some hosts, all that may be necessary to make the garden look lovely by party time is a morning spent weeding, raking, staking, and generally tidying up the plot. However, if you are holding a party outdoors for the first time or are hosting an elaborate event requiring special lighting or a sound system, it is a good idea to carefully consider the many possibilities for the party mood and setting before sending out the invitations. Remember, it is never too early to begin preparations for a garden party. You will need to plant and design your garden in advance, as well as research professional party services if you will need to hire help. Above all, do not be daunted by the plethora of garden styles and possibilities presented here. Your party, ultimately, will be your own event.

The Four-Season Garden

Your garden's best entertaining spot may very well move during the year, depending on what blooms where during each season. An overhanging tree that shelters a small luncheon party from the sun in midsummer also prevents an early spring sun from making its debut. Even the view from an established party spot will change as trees grow and lose leaves. Look carefully, with fresh eyes, at the views from various garden locations. Take some photographs to remind yourself of how a spot will look at a given time in the year. Hesitate before you plan a party near a rose bush that is busy with bees—and be aware that a tree that attracts bees in the spring will usually bring birds in the fall.

It is not possible to have all areas of the garden in top form for the entire year, so different spots should be focused on during different months. Veteran garden hosts and hostesses agree that the spots that will be most welcoming to your guests will almost always be those areas you naturally gravitate to with your cup of morning coffee or your afternoon iced tea on non-party days.

The grace of a well-tended garden is that it is never, no matter what the season, uninviting. Even in the snows of coldest winter, a stroll along a path, a mug of mulled cider in hand, can lift the heart. Yet for the gardener who delights in entertaining under the trees, the magic word—the awaited hour—is spring.

It is as early, perhaps, as mid-March that the day warms enough to beckon us out to the garden. At the end of a leisurely spring luncheon, three o'clock when the day is warmest, the sun demonstrates its sweet, seductive powers. The snowdrops and aconites are greeted, the moment is savored. Then a chill returns, but jacketed guests are pleased to have ventured into the expectant garden.

Many gardens are ideal for early spring plantings, perhaps on a south-facing slope adjoining the wall of a heated house. Such a spot can be created with a wall, a fence, windbreak of evergreens, or even a boulder to temper the wind and reflect the sun. Trees may have to be thinned to let early spring sunlight in, but remember that they will be leafless when these first spring blooms reach for the sun. Be careful, too, not to put forced buds outside too

© Wolfgang Kaehler

▲ Much-loved classics such as lily-of-the-valley (top) are a welcome sight to early springtime garden guests. Traditionally, the brave crocus (above) sends out the season's first invitation: "Look, the sun is warm, join me."

◄ The purple and yellow fanfare of salvia and yellowhammer are spring party decorations well worth your advance planning and care.

As they do today, aubretia and cordon apple greeted Monet and his early spring guests in the artist's Clos Normande garden (following page).

early, exposing them to the damaging effects of a late frost.

Not only spring's flowers—early scilla, galanthus, and crocus and their new green leaves—but its flowering trees provide delicious settings for garden entertaining with their delightful colors and fragrances. Many perennials bloom in early spring, even before the leaves of deciduous trees are fully developed.

At the height of spring, iris, tulip, narcissus, lily of the valley, and grape hyacinth are all in bloom, and the garden floor might be cloaked in a ground cover of tufted rock cresses. Climbing clematis and wisteria would be lovely touches to ornament a trellis surrounding a dining terrace.

The delicacy of the spring garden eventually gives way to the intensity of the full-flowering summer garden. "'Summer afternoon.' To me those have always been the two most beautiful words in the English language," said Henry James. It is in the months of June, July, and August, the time of deepening leaves, that the thoroughly warmed garden blossoms with hydrangea, the tree peony, roses, fuchsia, and much more. These are also months that benefit from your careful selection of annuals, chosen for their shapes and heights as well as their colors. The broad leaves of perennials such as hostas and daylilies can easily be used to conceal spring foliage's dying leaves.

The challenge of the summer garden is not to make flowers bloom, but to make a judicious selection of plants. So many flowers bloom in the summer months, it may be difficult to decide what to grow. But if the gardener does not address in advance this aspect of planning, the garden may take on a jumbled, haphazard look. One way to unite various plantings is to choose a color scheme. Pinks and yellows are always pleasing and have an air of romance about them—this would be an especially nice choice for a fragrant rose garden. Blue, silver, and lavender shades are especially popular for summer gardens, as they suggest water and sea breezes. If you live in a particularly warm climate or if your backyard receives an abundance of unimpeded sunlight, it is a good idea to invest in a retractable canopy to shield guests from sun or sun umbrellas fitted into dining tables. Seated in the shade with a cool drink in hand, guests will hardly notice the summer heat.

SPRING-FLOWERING TREES AND SHRUBS

Flowering trees and shrubs are another spectacular offering of spring. You are lucky if your garden includes a well-established tree or shrub. If it does not, you will enjoy adding one, and your guests will enjoy watching it develop over the years.

Dogwood
There are over 50 species of dogwood around the world, and 17 native to North America.

Cornus canadensis	zone 2	Bunchberry
Cornus alba 'Sibirica'	zone 2	Siberian dogwood
Cornus florida	zone 4	Flowering dogwood

Magnolia
Over 85 species to choose from, but these are our favorites.

Magnolia grandiflora	zone 7	Southern magnolia
Magnolia stellata	zone 5	Star magnolia

Cultivated Crabapple
There are 25 species of crabapple throughout the world, including *Malus pumila*, the parent of modern cultivated apple varieties.

Malus floribunda	zone 4	Japanese flowering crabapple
Malus sargentii	zone 4	Sargent crabapple

Note: Spring flowering shrubs and trees usually shed all their flowers in a few days. Try to notice from year to year when your shrubs or trees lose their lovely show so you will not plan your entertainments during that time next year.

© Derek Fell

◄ A weathered stone bench near a waterlilied pond will remind your visitors of Henry James' description of "summer afternoon," the two most beautiful words in the English language.

▼ Let your azalea help you decide when to host a party. Mark its time of full bloom on your garden calendar, and plan a cheerful celebration around those dates the following year.

© Richard Day

SUMMER-BLOOMING FLOWERS

July

Achillea filipendulina	zone 4	Yarrow
Lavandula angustifolia	zone 5	English lavender
Chrysanthemum parthenium	zone 4	Feverfew
Gypsophila paniculata	zone 3	Baby's breath
Chrysanthemum x superbum	zone 5	Shasta daisy
Antirrhinum majus	annual	Snapdragon
Zinnia elegans	annual	Zinnias
Coreopsis lanceolata	zone 4	Coreopsis
Celosia cristata	annual	Crested cockscomb
Cleome hasslerana	annual	Spiderflower
Phlox paniculata	zone 4	Phlox
Centaurea cyanus	annual	Bachelor's button
Rudbeckia fulgida	zone 4	Black-eyed Susan

August

Consolida ambigua	annual	Larkspur
Salvia splendens	annual	Scarlet Sage
Salvia farinacea	annual	Blue Salvia
Cosmos bipannatus	annual	Cosmos
Tagetes patula	annual	Marigold
Aster novae-angliae	zone 4	Michaelmas daisy
Lilium lancifolium	zone 4	Tiger lily
Echinops ritro	zone 3	Globe thistle
Eryngium giganteum	zone 5	Sea-holly
Heliopsis helianthoides	zone 4	False sunflower
Lisianthus russulanus	annual	Prairie Gentian

"The drowsy bee stumbles among the clover tops and summer sweetens all to me," said James Russell Lowell. This is the sweetest season in your garden, now overflowing with color and scent. Nothing has yet to ripen. Everything is in full bloom, everything planted and promised is there to be admired, clipped, tumbled into baskets, and sometimes enjoyed at the table. And a languid, candlelit summer evening is what memories are made of: the laughter of friends and the tinkling of ice caught up and carried off on a gentle summer breeze.

Fall's inspired foliage provides a grand setting for garden entertaining, but requires a bit of extra effort. The same brilliant reds and clear yellow leaves that dazzle us from their branches are slippery and dangerous on the ground and must be raked. But an artificially pristine garden is unsettling, too. Sen no Rikyu of sixteenth-century Japan still felt dissatisfied after he swept and tidied his garden. So he shook the maple tree and two or three flaming leaves fell on the mossy ground.

Berry-bearing shrubs also provide autumn garden color. Cotoneasters, pyracantha, and hollies provide a show of red and orange berries; viburnums and some dogwoods bear bluish or black berries. Some of the rose bushes that dazzled garden visitors with flowers in summer are ornamented in autumn with rosehips in many shades of red and some in black. And the seedpods and seedheads of many plants create sculptural accents in the garden. An orderly but rustic autumn garden is perhaps most enjoyable during hors d'oeuvres and cocktails and after dinner, with a cozy house providing the main meal setting.

The Japanese consider snow to be the floral display of winter, as evidenced by the many photographs and paintings of Japanese

◄▲ Do you invite friends to your garden after summer fades? Offer them a red carpet of maple leaves. Careful, though; test the path first to make sure it is not slippery.

◄ This garden is in Pennsylvania, not Kyoto, but everyone will welcome the chance to stroll through its tranquil whiteness or to view it from a picture window. Someone understood the winter possibilities of this garden enough to place an oriental stone lantern near the pond.

© Derek Fell

SNOW-BLOOMING PLANTS

Shrubs

Lonicera fragrantissima	zone 5	Winter honeysuckle
Hamamelis x *intermedia*	zone 5	Witch hazel
H. mollis	zone 5	Chinese witch hazel
H. vernalis	zone 4	Vernal witch hazel
Jasminum nudiflorum	zone 5	Winter jasmine
Lindera benzoin	zone 4	Spicebush

Bulbs

Galanthus elwesii	zone 5	Giant snowdrops
Crocus vernus	zone 4	Crocus
Scilla siberica	zone 2–3	Siberian Squill
Eranthis hyemalis	zone 4	Winter Aconite

Perennials

Helleborus niger	zone 3	Christmas-rose
H. orientalis	zone 6	Lenten-rose
H. lividus	zone 7	Corsica Christmas-rose

WINTER FLOWERS

Force these fragrant bulbs to add color and scent to your wintertime garden parties. Be careful, though; their lovely odor may bring on bouts of spring fever among your guests.

Narcissus triandrus	zone 4	Angel's tears
Hyacinthus orientalis	zone 4	Common hyacinth
Hippeastrum hybrida	zone 9	Amaryllis
Colchicum speciosum	zone 5	Crocus

© John N. Trager/Visuals Unlimited

CHRISTMAS TREES AND HOLIDAY DECORATIONS

Any garden entertainer who has a holiday party will probably prefer a living Christmas tree to a cut one. After the spring, plant the tree in your garden.

Pseudotsuga menziesii	zone 4–6	Douglas fir
Pinus sylvestris	zone 2	Scotch pine
Abies fraseri	zone 4	Fraser fir

Boughs, swags, and wreaths are most beautiful and longest lasting when they are made from Scotch pine or Easter white pine (*Pinus strobus*).

Poinsettias (*Euphorbia pulcherrima*) are a perennial holiday favorite. They can be easily transplanted to the garden and encouraged to bloom again if they are cut back hard after their holiday flowering is finished. However, remember that poinsettias are poisonous. The sap released after cutting is a skin irritant, and the leaves are harmful if eaten. This may not be a problem for your guests, but keep an eye on your pets.

Another intriguing holiday season plant is a Christmas cactus (*Schlumbergera truncata*). Christmas cosmos (*Montanoa hibiscifolia*) is another December-blooming plant that should be used to bring the garden inside to your holiday parties.

gardens mantled softly in white. Take a cue from the wise gardeners of Japan, and consider your winter garden a treasure to be designed and viewed from inside the house, as well as to be enjoyed from its snowy pathways.

Inside lighting controls give the winter gardener a great opportunity to dramatize the outdoors, to make it a second party room as seen from inside the house. This is particularly effective if you have a porch that can be glassed-in during cold weather. But remember that it will not always be covered with snow. If the winter garden tends toward brown grass and bare trees, then augment with evergreens, conifers, ivies, rhododendrons, junipers with foliage ranging from yellow, gray, and blue.

Winter colors are not limited to greens and blues either. Japanese crytomeria (*Cryptomeria japonica* 'Elegans') turns a rich red-brown in winter. Winterberry (*Ilex verticillata*) presents bright red berries that last through the winter. Winter bloom (*Hamamelis virginiana*) blooms late into the year with glorious bright yellow flowers. Kerria (*Kerria japonica*) carries bright green stems through the winter, while Siberian Dogwood (*Cornus alba* 'Sibirica') offers bright red bark.

Many types of autumn cherry, winter-sweet, winter forsythia, iris, crocus, winter jasmine, daffodil, garden pansy, anemone, snowdrop, rhododendron, hepatica, and cyclamen will provide fresh, colorful blooms when they are most needed. However, before planting look through the window from the inside of your house to ensure that you are not planning on placing a large bush right in the middle of the view.

Experienced winter gardeners often heighten the seasonal experience by placing fragrant plants near the back and front doors, so their scents enter the house with each guest.

The garden, whatever the time of year, is never closed or inaccessible to the partying viewer, whether observed from inside or out. There is no "off season." The garden never has a "down time," but can always be relied upon to enhance or enchant a gathering. The garden is always busy changing, working with nature to show us its wonders, speaking to us as long as we take the time to listen and learn its ways.

◀◀ Japanese cedar in two shades of green lends a perfect flavor to a holiday party in your garden.

▼ The Japanese, unfailingly wise in the ways of winter, say that snow graces winter branches as beautifully as blossoms do—and so this dogwood enjoys a second flowering.

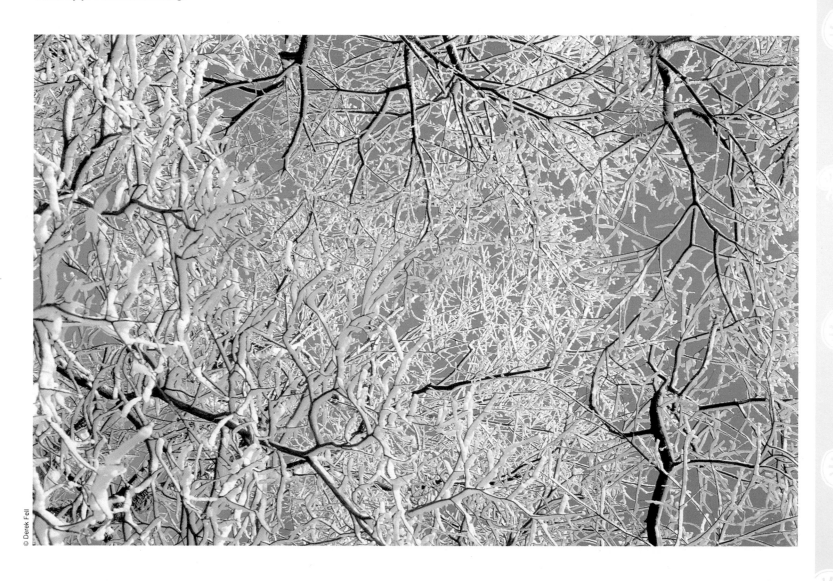

◄ To accent whatever is flowering at party time, gather containers of lavish blooms into abundant groupings around a window, a doorway, or an archway.

© Derek Fell

►▲ Serenity is not found in empty spaces, but rather in simplicity: A weather-worn stone from the garden and a simple potted red geranium are gently framed by a wall alcove.

© Nancy Hill

Garden Styles

Depending on the size of your property and the mode in which you wish to entertain, your garden can be a vast, fully blooming plot with the capacity to entertain many guests or a small private space perfect for intimate dinner parties. Here are some ideas for making any size garden a showplace.

The Mini-Garden

Among serious British estate gardeners, any plot less than an acre is small; some European grounds are so expansive that a kitchen garden alone is over an acre. Of course, such vast gardens are only possible with hired help and many hours of care.

Today, gardening is becoming a popular pastime for people with modest yards, and small, cozy gardens are the norm. The joy of tending them is part of having them.

If you do not have a cultivated garden and would like the opportunity to entertain outdoors, consider creating a small jewel-box within a hedge, a wall, a fence, or even set off by a change of ground level. You might use only flowering plants and paving materials for this small but inviting area. A limited selection of stunning flowers takes only a few hours to plant and tend, yet will provide many hours of enjoyment. When you entertain, place tables on the lawn near this mini-garden. This arrangement creates the feeling of a charming outdoor cafe.

Container Gardening

A lack of outdoor space doesn't mean you have to do without a garden. With container gardening you don't even need ground; enough plants in pots will give you a garden to go. Even fruit trees grow well in containers when they are kept inside during every season but summer.

Aside from the classic clay and glazed ceramic pots, there are many creative ways to decorate your deck, your backyard, your steps, your terrace, and your walkway with blooming color. A clay pipe set on end, an old wheelbarrow, a wicker chair, or even a burlap bag of potting soil with slits for the plants will welcome your guests. If it is a balcony or a roof you are using, be sure it is structurally sound before weighing it down with heavy pots.

It is important to remember that container gardening requires a soilless mix such as peat moss or shredded bark with perlite or vermiculite. Potted plants also require good drainage and frequent watering. A large succulent plant, such as a geranium with foliage overflowing its container's sides, will take as much as twenty ounces of water on a bright, sunny day. And more than fifty percent of the water evaporates from clay pots. Mulching the soil surface will help lessen evaporation.

The clear advantage to container gardening is the spontaneous decorating you can do with your plants, moving them at your whim, to suit your mood and the needs of your guests.

The more weathered a garden container, the more distinguished it looks. New growth seems to burst out of this cement pot.

Carefully placed potted geraniums, enhanced by overflowing spider plants, mark the path to this bathhouse, and add color accents to the grey slate ledges and green plantings.

Do not give up your dream of entertaining in your garden just because it is a space with difficult constraints. Both of these gardens display creative designs that make the most of challenging settings. The garden on the left is not only in the middle of a city, but it is also in a deeply shaded spot. The designer carefully chose plantings—mostly ivies—suited to the microclimate. The trellis and the flagstone path leading to the bench give the viewer a feeling of height and depth. The small garden above, designed by Helene Heyning, also moves up rather than out. The ivy-covered walls and the subtle curve of the abundant border plantings soften the boundaries of this small area. Few people would guess that the door at the back of the garden leads to the hustle and bustle of New York City.

The Night Garden

The enjoyment of the garden by night is much more a part of Chinese and Japanese life than of Western culture. There are world-famous Oriental pavilions especially built for viewing the moon or gazing at the plum blossom by moonlight. Night garden viewing, as a matter of fact, is one of the four most popular pursuits of Japanese vacationers. The Japanese even create structures and "seas" of white sand specifically for their moon-reflecting properties.

Western night gardens, with judicious planning, will please from inside the house, looking out, or from inside the garden itself. Night-blooming plants set a dramatic scene, whether planted in the earth or in moveable pots. Even gray-leafed plants have a luminescent effect on blue flowers. Light-colored periwinkles, lilies, impatiens, and caladiums, white rhododendrons and azaleas all seem to shine at night.

If you are planting a night garden it is important to remember that some beautiful daytime plants will retreat into shadow at night. Many deep purples, blues, reds, and even oranges will disappear after sundown.

However, a dark background of plantings or structure is important to showcase night bloomers, along with white structures that reflect night lighting. All-white gardens are always impressive, whether viewed at dawn, dusk, or midnight. "I love color, rejoice in it, but white is lovely to me forever," wrote Vita Sackville-West, the twentieth-century British garden writer and

Sweeping vistas of light-catching plants promise a garden that will not fade when moonlight replaces sun.

novelist whose white garden at Sissinghurst, England, is an undisputed classic. Its pristine tree peonies and climbing roses create the atmosphere of an enchanted bower. These "make a dream of the garden, an unreal vision, yet one knows that it isn't unreal at all because one has planted it all for effect."

Whatever their color, place night-bloomers along garden walkways, especially if they give off a pleasant scent, such as fragrant jasmines. Some special plants are not only well suited to be celebration settings, but are themselves cause to celebrate. Each year a Connecticut family plans an intimate cocktail party around the ephemeral life of their night-blooming Cereus. This beloved plant is more applauded in its brief existence than many taken-for-granted perennials.

Lady Sarashina's eleventh century words describe
a peaceful night in the garden:
The hazy Springtime moon—
That is the one I love,
When light green sky and fragrant blooms
Are all alike enwrapped in mist.

© Balthazar Korab

Include a white flowering tree in a garden to create an enchanted bower in moonlight, making what Vita Sackville-West called "a dream of a garden, an unreal vision" for the delight of nighttime visitors. This dogwood glows at night and shades a cheerful table of daytime guests as well.

▶ If you desire a night-white garden, or just a section, be sure to provide seating nearby, with perhaps a subtle accent to draw the eye, such as a birdhouse.

▶▶ A garden is a time-free zone. One of the few reminders of the days and hours that is welcome here is the stately sundial.

THE MOONLIT GARDEN

White blooms will catch moonlight and send it sparkling back to the viewer. Add some of these flowers to your garden, and it will always dazzle your nighttime guests.

Cosmos bipinnatus	annual	Cosmos
Nicotiana alata	annual	Flowering Nightshade
Petunia x *hybrida*	annual	Petunia
Polianthus tuberosa	zone 9	Tuberose
Anemone hupehensis japonica	zone 5	Japanese anemone
Aster dumosus 'Snowy Cushion'	zone 2–3	Bushy aster
Gypsophila paniculata	zone 2–3	Baby's breath
Iberis sempervirens 'Snowflake'	zone 3	Candytuft
Chrysanthemum morifolium	zone 5	Chrysanthemum
Ipomoea quamolit var. *alba*	annual	Cypress vine

© Derek Fell

© Derek Fell

GARDEN ACCENTS

The plants and their organization in each garden distinguishes their garden's style from any other. Garden accents are the accessories that enhance these natural themes.

Japanese gardens: stone lanterns, bamboo fences, silent Buddha, granite bases

Victorian gardens: gazebos, wooden benches, hot house, conservatories, statues

Colonial gardens: sundial, beeskeep

Wildlife gardens: birdbath, birdhouse, feeders

Secret gardens: fence gate with a key

Medieval gardens: images of unicorns, tributes to saints

Children's gardens: stone animals, such as rabbits, frogs, and turtles

Farmer's gardens: wheelbarrels planted with herbs

© R.F. Wilson

Guest Amenities

Unless it is neglected—though you can remedy that—your garden is the perfect place for a party. The plants and grounds may have to be tidied, just as your living room would, but today the only rules governing gardens as a place for entertaining are those ensuring hospitality and safety.

It was not always so. Eleventh–century Japanese consulted an official book before they laid out their gardens. They believed that if the regulations for the placing of stone benches or washing places were broken, "the owner will sicken unto death, his residence shall also be laid waste, and shall become as the dwelling place of demons."

Today the best preparation for a season of garden entertaining is common sense, care, and a feeling that what is right to you is right for your guests. With that attitude you will be comfortable in your own garden, and so will your guests.

When you take a party outside, you must expect some creatures other than your guests to join you, and some will be more welcome than others. Among the visitors you will surely want in your warm weather garden are butterflies, ladybugs, hummingbirds, and other signs of garden health and vitality. One way to ensure high level company is to avoid using commercial insecticides and fungicides. Many successful gardeners learn which species or varieties of plants attract insects or disease and choose those that are bred for resistance. Your human guests will be happier in a chemical-free environment, as well, especially if they are prone to sampling vegetables and herbs from your food garden.

Seaside and other breezy garden locations, of course, are blessed with bug-free evenings, but mosquitoes are often a very big problem in other areas. The most common and benign solution is citronella candles, available in many sizes. Hosts should place insect repellant sprays and liquids in the powder rooms of their houses. Women may be advised to not leave legs bare and all guests to wear long sleeves and pants. A selection of jackets might be kept on hand for anti-mosquito reasons as well as protection from cold. On warm evenings, a low-speed fan aimed at the area where guests are congregating can discourage mosquitoes.

For use during the day, wire mesh food protectors are available to protect food from flies. Some partygivers do not bring the food out until last minute. In Europe, marigolds and geraniums are grown because they are said to repel flies. Flowers that attract bees and wasps should never be grown near dining areas. A sting to a highly sensitive guest could mean a trip to the hospital.

© Derek Fell

◄ Careful garden planning should guarantee that over-hanging plants do not attract bees or interfere with walking, that latticework and seating is freshly painted and free of splinters, and that ponds are fresh and fragrant. It is wise to meander your own pathways as if you never have before, perhaps at dusk or early morn, to make sure there are no misplaced bricks or stones that would cause guests to stumble.

© Derek Fell

BUTTERFLY ATTRACTORS

Flitting butterflies will add romance and beauty to your garden, so you will want them coming around. They are attracted to plants with large flower heads, upon which they can land. Here is a list of some of the best attractors.

Flowers

Lobularia maritima	annual	Sweet alyssum
Borago officinalis	annual	Borage
Heliotropium arborenscens	zone 10	Heliotrope
Lantana camara	zone 8	Lantana
Tropaeolum majus	annual	Nasturtium
Matthiola incana	annual	Stock
Aster novae-angliae	zone 2–3	New England aster
Asclepias tuberosa	zone 3	Butterfly milkweed
Rosmarinus officinalis	zone 6	Rosemary
Echinacea purpurea	zone 3	Echinacea
Coreopsis grandiflora	zone 7	Coreopsis
Hemerocallis spp.	zone 2–3	Daylily
Baptisia tinctoria	zone 5–6	Wild indigo
Dictamnus albus	zone 2–3	Gasplant
Alcea rosea	zone 2–3	Hollyhock
Lythrum salicaria	zone 3	Loosestrife
Sedum spectabile	zone 3	Sedum

Shrubs

Buddleia alternifolia	zone 5	Fountain buddleia
Buddleia davidii	zone 5	Butterfly bush
Syringa vulgaris	zone 3	Lilac
Wisteria floribunda	zone 4	Wisteria

© Derek Fell

BEE ATTRACTORS

Before you have a party, make sure that you organized
activities away from flowers, trees, or shrubs that attract
bees and wasps. Here is a list of plants to keep an eye on;
most of these are only an attraction when in bloom.

Trees

Alnus rhombifolia	zone 5	White alder
Betula species	zone 3	Birch
Crataegus species	zone 4	Hawthorne
Eucalyptus species	zone 10	Gum
Liriodendron tulipifera	zone 4	Tulip tree
Malus species	zone 3–4	Crabapple
Populus species	zone 2–5	Aspen
Cornus species	zone 3–7	Dogwood

Shrubs

Berberis species	zone 4–7	Barberry
Cytisus species	zone 5–8	Broom
Fuchsia species	zone 5–10	Fuchsia
Pyracantha species	zone 5–8	Firethorn
Rhus species	zone 2–10	Sumac
Syringa species	zone 2–5	Lilac
Viburnum species	zone 2–9	Viburnam

Flowers

Aconitum species	zone 2–5	Monk's hood
Armeria maritima	zone 3	Seathrift
Allium schoenoprasum	zone 2–3	Chives
Delphinium species	annual	Larkspur
Digitalis species	zone 3–4	Foxglove
Campanula rotundifolia	zone 2–3	Bluebells
Echinops species	zone 3–4	Globe thistle
Primula species	zone 2–7	Primrose
Narcissus species	zone 2–7	Daffodil

HUMMINGBIRD ATTRACTORS

Busy hummingbirds are a fascinating guest in any
garden. They are attracted to red flowers and flowers
they can hover near. Try growing some of these and
you will soon be hosting feathered friends along
with human ones.

Salvia splendens	annual	Scarlet sage
Antirrhinum majus	annual	Snapdragon
Aquilegia canadensis	zone 2–3	Columbine
Monarda didyma	zone 4	Bee-balm
Heuchera sanguinea	zone 3	Coral-bell
Lupinus pubescens	annual	Lupine
Phlox paniculata	zone 4	Phlox
Hibiscus moscheutos	zone 5	Rose mallow

Preparty Garden Renovations

Observing your garden with new eyes, as if you were a guest, is essential if you are not going to overlook any element in your preparty planning. Is there an eyesore you have adjusted to, though a first-time guest will not so easily overlook it? Is there an unattractive road or highway you have become accustomed to? A well-placed arbor, latticework, swathed in leafy, blooming plants or palm fronds may conceal it. The common wisteria, for instance, which will grow in the sun against latticework or a trellis, will reach a height of six feet (183 cm). The shrubby June-berry tree, also known as serviceberry, will grow to twelve feet (366 cm), and promise profuse mid-spring flowers, lush young leaves, and brilliant autumn foliage. A combination of lilac and mock orange will beautifully conceal a tool shed, the pump house, or garbage cans. The possibilities are inspiring.

If the eyesore is on your own property, easily grown climbers will make a substantial covering over old trees, walls, or sheds. *Clematis paniculata* will reach forty feet (12 m) and offer fragrant white flowers as well. Ultrahardy lilacs reach twelve feet (3.6 m), as do wisteria, dogwood, and many others. Beans trained up poles and grapes trained in a fan shape along a trellis make fine coverups, too, if planted early enough.

Evergreens are the key to shelter when other limbs are bare. The distinguished Renaissance gardener John Evelyn wrote that the evergreen "defends both our Gardens and the dwelling from the penetration of the winds and the extremities of the weather. And verily an ingenious Gardiner may so invirone his enclosures and Avenues, with Verdures that they shall seem to be placed in one of the Summer Ilands and to enjoy an Eternal Spring, when all the rest of the country is bared and naked." Evelyn may have overstated the case, but the point is well taken.

To offer protection in areas of high wind, plant conifers close together so that even when the plants are young, they will still afford protection from wind and create a privacy screen. The evergreens that function handsomely as windbreaks also control snow drift and provide habitats for small animals and birds in the Midwest and Great Plains. There's a name for the Midwest's

A meandering stream through a perennial garden will surely attract butterflies and guests—and perhaps stinging insects as well, unless you plan carefully (preceding page).

◄◄ As the name implies, butterfly bush attracts beautiful flitting friends; it also blooms all summer, unlike most shrubs, which show in spring.

▼ These may not be very attractive walls, as walls go, and they would make a less-than-successful party "room," but English ivy transforms them into traditional areas of cool distinction.

© Derek Fell

staggered methods of planting their evergreens for wind and snow control: a shelterbelt. Such windbreaks should be placed at right angles to the wind for most effective use.

Grooming the Pre-party Garden

Don't be overwhelmed by a garden that seems to be in a state of embarrassing disrepair. In 1930, one Englishwoman began to clean up seven acres of "old bedsteads, old ploughshares, old cabbage stalks, old broken-down earth closets, old matted wire, and mountains of sardine tins, all muddled up in a tangle of Bindweed, Nettles and Ground Elder." Under the hand of the undaunted gardener, Vita Sackville-West, that trash heap became the world-famous garden at Sissinghurst Castle.

In the gardening world, "deadhead" means more than a guest you wish you had not invited. It is the act of cleaning dead blossoms and leaves from otherwise healthy plants, and it is something you will want to give a good deal of time to before guests arrive. Annuals require deadheading several times a week. Deadheading encourages new growth, especially with perennials.

Though your garden's charm may lie in its well-in-hand wildness, look at it with a barber's eye. Does anything distract you from the whole by fleeing its border? Is anything disconcertingly tall or short? Do not feel you have to waste any cuttings you may glean from this cleanup work. There are vases and bowls waiting to be filled with each barbered bloom.

Out-of-control shrubs can mean the loss of natural pathways as well as the possibility of fungus and rot forming under the shaded hedgerows of plantings gone wild. Keeping down weeds, another important pre-party necessity, also helps to control garden diseases in general.

Caring for your guests means that you must prune thorny plantings till they are well out of walkways. Not only eye-level plantings must be groomed, but foot-level as well. Walk through your garden at night and see if you are impeded at any point. Clip roots that are stumbling blocks. If you cannot, cover them with sod and light the areas around them very well so that the mounded section will not be hazardous to walkers.

© Derek Fell

The sharp-eyed host or hostess will not allow a creeping juniper—with its reliable year-round freshness—to creep beyond reasonable limits. Trim its wildness during pre-party preparations (far left, top).

An unassuming white garden fence becomes a dramatic focal point when topped with a lavish tumbling of colorful bougainvillea (far left, center).

A fence that is creatively designed certainly does not need disguising; it will, instead, serve as an effective frame or display area for the colorful summer blooms that climb it and those in its vicinity (far left, bottom).

◄ A strategically placed cedar will afford both privacy and an amazing amount of windbreak to the entertaining garden, along with a fresh, unfailing greenness.

Check for loose flagstones; secure them. Mortar, if necessary, well in advance so the patch has time to dry.

Looking around with new eyes, you may very well see areas where more or different plantings are called for. Do not let bare spaces in your garden be a cause for alarm. Gertrude Jekyll, known as "The Beautifier of England" and one of the greatest gardeners in the Western world, wrote that three months was the maximum span for a border to look very well, and that it was "quite unreasonable" to expect anything else. "It can only be done where there are the means of having large reserves of material that can be planted or plunged in the borders to take the place of plants gone out of bloom. Owners of gardens should clearly understand that this is so—acceptance of the fact would save them from much fruitless effort and inevitable disappointment." The no-nonsense Miss Jekyll, who groomed her exquisitely natural garden in army boots and an old apron, grants you permission to expect holes and to fill them in as you will.

Filling in "holes" in your garden landscape is easily achieved with containers. The more imaginative the pots, the more fun they are for your guests to admire. The lighter they are, the easier they are for you to move into spots where they are needed, whether on a porch or where a plant has run its course.

Scrap metal dealers, building supply yards, and junkyards are good places to pick up pipes, blocks, flue tiles in which to plant. Flea markets and yard sales should be watched for pickle crocks or blue-speckled washtubs. Such containers look attractive with plants cascading down the sides, as well.

Maintaining the Lawn

Lawns sometimes develop unsightly thin or weak areas because of disease, temperature stress, and/or insect infestations. Lawn repair products are available that contain grass seed, a moisture retaining ingredient and agents—organic, ideally—to encourage faster germination. This system starts new grass in six to seven days, depending on the type of grass. Bare spots should fill in completely in three to four weeks. If you are simply reseeding, be sure to cover the spots with a light mulch to hold the seed in

© Beverly G. Bowe

HOW TO
PRUNE YOUR GARDEN

To maintain proper production and size,
pinch, disbud, and deadhead your flowering
plants as often as every other day. Pinch a
small amount of the plant's growing tip to
encourage a sturdier, fuller, more compact
growth and discourage leggy tendrils.
Disbud the plant's alternate buds to force
the remaining buds to produce larger, more
prominent, and more evenly spaced flowers.
Deadhead all spent flowers during the
season to promote new buds to form; pinch
off the wilted flowers about
two inches (5 cm) down the stem.

Guests who stroll, drinks in hand, along this
manicured hedge-and-tulip border will have no
dead leaves or blossoms, no stray twigs to distract them from the beauty at hand and the
happy expectation of the supper to come.

◄ This swath of grass serves as both lawn and walkway, so it has been specially seeded with a hardier grass. It is checked before each gathering for stones and holes that might trip strolling guests.

◄ ▼ A weathered arbor with seats is most welcome at path's end, offering shade, rest, and a bit of an old-fashioned feeling to the unwinding, pre-dinner garden guest.

► ► The antique urn discreetly displays its flowering plants, while the fountain leads the eye to the water beyond. These are examples of terrace accoutrements that do not distract from, but rather enhance the area's natural beauty.

place. Spring and late summer are the times to do this.

If you prefer to sod, which produces an instant lawn even in winter, rather than seed, choose only good quality sod with a lush, uniform color and a thick-bodied cut. Check carefully to see that thatch—a tightly intermingled layer of living and dead stems, leaves and roots of grasses—is minimal in the sod you buy.

Water your lawn well ahead of your party, so it will be dry enough to walk on. Test it for dryness the week before: How dry is it one day after watering, two days, and so on? And, while cuttings can generally benefit your lawn, they will stick to the shoes of garden party guests and should be taken up right before the party.

The Lawn Institute in Pleasant Hill, Tennessee, advises homeowners to ignore the lush photograph on the grass seed package and read the label carefully. Varieties of bluegrass or fescue that are given names are new, improved varieties that have superior traits to the common, unnamed, or generic types. They are more attractive, more disease- and insect-resistant, and give more value. Annual ryegrass, for instance, is a frequent component of inexpensive seed mixtures. It sprouts quickly but generally will not survive into the second year. If it does, it becomes coarse and clumpy. A small amount of annual ryegrass, though, can be useful as a companion grass where quick cover is needed to protect a newly seeded slope.

For a lawn free of dandelions, cut the plants two to four inches (½ to 1 cm) below the crown to reduce regrowth. Digging or pulling out weeds is easier after a heavy rain or watering.

Garden Accoutrements

Pay careful attention to the accoutrements of your garden setting —the paths, steps, seats, lighting and sound systems, and other atmosphere enhancers. Of course, the plants, flowers, trees, and shrubs of your garden should take center stage. Let these other accessories emphasize your guests' enjoyment of the beautiful and peaceful setting nature has created with your help.

Plan carefully when you are selecting garden accoutrements.

Find the best spots in your garden and choose appointments to enhance these spots, not detract from their natural beauty. Set a bench across from a hummingbird-attracting bush, so your guests can watch without disturbing the birds. Use a path to lure your friends to a particularly beautiful, but secluded corner of the garden. Use lighting to dramatize the garden at night, to highlight trees, bushes, or plants that may be missed during the day. Add music to soothe the nerves even further; while nature offers peace and beauty to the eyes and nose, technology calms the ears.

More important, however, make certain that your garden accents appear as an indigenous part of the setting and mood you have created. No guest should stumble over an uneven stone in a path or trip on a too-low step. A bench should be a place to rest and contemplate, so place it in a secluded spot, but not under a messy tree or too close to a noisy area.

Every accoutrement has its own special considerations and contributions. No one understands these issues better than the professionals who help design garden settings everywhere. Listen to the advice and insight gleaned from these expert garden appointers, here and in Part Two: Advice from Professionals and Partygivers. Their wisdom and experience will help you create the most beautiful garden possible.

© Derek Fell

POOR TREES FOR GARDEN ENTERTAINING

If you have chosen to treat your garden as a special place to entertain, you will want to make sure that none of the plants interfere. Here is a list of trees that could cause problems for you and your guests.

Acer negundo   Box elder
Weedy; hosts box-elder bugs

Aesculus hippocastanum   Horsechestnut
Weedy; weak wood breaks easily; male flowers carry a foul smell

Aralia elata   Japanese angelica
Prickly stems with thorns; invasive root suckers

Betula populifolia   Gray birch
Weak wood breaks easily; leaf miners disfigure leaves

Juglans nigra   Eastern black walnut
Messy; fruit stains ground; roots secrete substance toxic to other plants

Robinia pseudoacacia   Black locust
Ages poorly; susceptible to borers, leaf miners, and other pests; bark is poisonous if eaten

Prunus virginiana   Choke cherry
Produces messy fruit; hosts tent caterpillars

Ulmus americana   American elm
Very susceptible to Dutch Elm Disease

Everything about this Charleston rose garden makes it an ideal setting for a party: fragrant blossoms of different colors and an arbor leading a guest onto a well-defined, interestingly curved, carefully maintained path. One word of caution: Overhanging roses should be checked regularly for dangerous thorns.

© Derek Fell

FRAGRANT PLANTS

The following plants will scent your garden deliciously. Be careful, when planning the smells of your garden, that the scents from the different plants do not clash or overwhelm each other. Plant the fragrant plants far enough away from each other, or make sure that they bloom or release their scents at different times of the day or season.

Lilium spp.	zone 3–7	Lily
Buddleia davidii	zone 5	Butterfly bush
Centaurea imperialis	annual	Royal centaurea
Clematis spp.	zone 4–7	Clematis
Dianthus spp.	zone 2–8	Carnation
Gardenia jasminoides	zone 8–9	Gardenia
Jasminum spp.	zone 5–10	Jasmine
Lavandula spp.	zone 5	Lavender
Muscari spp.	zone 2–8	Hyacinth
Stephanotis floribunda	zone 10	Stephanotis
Wisteria sinensis	zone 5	Wisteria
Citrus spp.	zone 10	Citrus tree
Laurus nobilis	zone 7	Sweet bay laurel

NIGHTTIME FRAGRANT PLANTS

Rosa var.	zone 2–7	Rose
Oenothera odorata	annual	Primrose
Datura metel	annual	Hindu datura
Echinops exaltatus	zone 3	Globe thistle
Freesia x hybrida	zone 9	Freesia
Pelargonium x fragens	zone 10	Geranium
Rosmarinus officinalis	zone 6	Rosemary
Hylocereus undatus	zone 10	Nightblooming Cereus

Pathways

Pathways can be designed however you like and should lend a consistent character to the entertaining garden. A path does a great deal to determine your garden's mood.

Even when you are not entertaining, you will be able to put a carefully planned garden walkway to good use, since it will provide easy access to your plants. A well-executed path also offers many gifts to the garden visitor. While your guests would not wander through your house during an indoor party, they will be expecting—night or day—to stroll through your garden, to stop, linger, then return to the dining area, and then perhaps to wander through again. That is the joy of being on a garden path.

Paths can take any imaginable form, whether made of brick, aggregate material, concrete, flagstone, grass, wood, or stepping stones. Typically, Roman gardens had carefully arranged walks, with a promenade both sheltered and sunny in winter, offering shade in summer and varieties of views. The promenade was a major feature of the Greek garden, where the philosophers gathered to ply their trade. And, of course, the traditional Oriental pathway is exquisitely thought out to provide a peaceful, inspired experience, during which the features of the garden unfold slowly. In such a garden, even the texture of the stones is taken into account in the design process.

This leisurely effect can be duplicated by designing graceful curves into a garden walkway. If the walkway is still in the planning stages, consider experimenting with the effects of irregular curves. Use a garden hose to establish experimental walkway lines. Straight walks look best with flower borders that spill over the edges, as in Monet's garden at Giverny. A focal point—statuary, a fountain, or sundial—can function as a garden walkway destination. Many gardeners feel that no pathway should be without such a destination.

Paths made from soft, natural materials are often the most inviting to guests seeking respite in a welcoming garden. This is one of the reasons that wood chips are popular today; additionally, they perform a valuable mulching function. Any number of natural materials can be used on pathways. Virginia Woolf once described a famous path that rambles through the Kensington Gardens:

> "That was one of the pleasures of scrunching the shells with which now and then the Flower Walk was strewn. They had little ribs in them like the shells on the beach."

Paths meant to be trod upon might very well be planted with fragrant covers, such as mint or thyme, so their scents waft up and greet the guest with a surprise gift. Sir Francis Bacon, the garden-loving philosopher of Renaissance England, described thyme as something that will "perfume the air most delightfully, not passed by as the rest, but being trodden upon and crushed." Thyme is said to be the sweet-scented carpet on which Shakespeare's fairy queen Titania rested and dreamed.

Some gardeners use mixed media in path design, employing such natural materials as a clay-and-pebble mixture, and punctuat-

ing the beginning and ending of paths with one carefully selected stepping-stone. This has the same effect as a door sill, conveying the sense that the visitor has left one world and entered another.

Be aware that the garden path should be broad enough for your guests' comfort. An entry path should be four to five feet (1.2 to 1.5 m) wide, enough to accommodate two people walking abreast, and wider if it is against the house or a wall. Actual garden walks can be as narrow as thirty inches (76 cm) wide, though thirty-six inches (90 cm) is more comfortable.

Before any gathering, inspect your walkway to see if there are areas that do not drain well. If drainage is a problem, add a gravel-filled ditch underneath walkway materials. It may be a good idea to walk your paths at dusk, paying attention to spots that may trip up a visitor. Patching should be done well in advance of the party, so a patching medium has had a chance to dry securely.

Try to imagine the "traffic patterns" that will develop in your garden. How will people get from place to place? Where will they most want to go? Always be aware that those you entertain

▲ ◀ In a formal New Jersey shrub garden, an appropriately elegant brick path, subtly varicolored, leads strollers to a point of interest and back again.

▲ Pebbles are comfortably crunchy as walking material in this Oregon garden. They also help to control weeds.

◀ ◀ With everything planned—rushes of color, borders overhanging, enough height to entertain the eye—the spring garden assumes an abundant, spontaneous look as it awaits its guests.

© Derek Fell

These natural wood-and-grass garden steps are not only a delight to walk on, but make ideal perches for conversing guests. Natural steps such as these do not separate garden areas as much as they link them. They also join guests, as they are wide enough for two people to stroll together, creating what designer Lisa Stamm calls "a garden that flows."

might not be wearing the kind of shoes one can leave in the mud room, so safe and dry areas must be provided.

Well-chosen paving takes on even greater importance in winter. When plants are dormant during cold months, a strong structure of paving, trees, and walls will be so effective that the absence of bloom will be far less noticeable.

Steps

Steps may separate a patio, terrace, or deck from a garden or divide levels within a garden. They should be wide and generous, with protected sides. Long flights should be broken up with a landing every eight to ten steps. The risers—the vertical measurement—should not be so high that it is an effort to walk up or down, and they must be of equal heights to prevent tripping. Garden steps may be far apart, but they should be spaced evenly. Risers of six or seven inches (15 cm or 17 cm) high and treads— the place where you step—of between ten and twelve inches (25 cm and 30 cm) wide, are the most comfortable, with a tread of fifteen inches (37 cm) being ideal. If the riser is lower, the tread should be proportionately wider; for instance, a four-inch (10-cm) riser and a nineteen-inch (48-cm) tread, or a five-inch (12-cm) riser and a seventeen-inch (42-cm) tread. Steps five feet (1.5 m) wide make it easy for two people to walk side by side. Broad garden steps make excellent impromptu seats for garden parties and serve as planter areas, if space permits.

Owners of a much-admired house and garden on New York's Shelter Island, Lisa Stamm and her husband, Dale Booher, an architect, use the design principles they have learned to enhance the garden entertaining they love. "The garden must flow from the house," explains Stamm. "It's important that you not have to step down into it. Notice how you react to a store in the city that is only one step below street level. Chances are you pass it by. When I do land designs I try, whenever possible, to create a garden that flows, where there is no step down." If steps are necessary, wide treads with low risers will help to maintain a flow.

The flow of a party can also be planned, Stamm has learned. "If you want people to gravitate to a pretty spot or to a table far

Garden, garden everywhere, even between the flagstones of your path. Planting such fragrant herbs as thyme or rosemary in the walk ensures that your guests are entranced by delightful scents.

GROUNDCOVERS FOR PATHS OR BETWEEN PATHSTONES

Your guests will be enchanted by the wafts of soft scent that rise to them as they walk along your garden path.

Thymus vulgaris	zone 5	Thyme
T. x citriodorus	zone 5	Lemon thyme
Galium odoratum	zone 4	Sweet woodruff
Rosmarinus officinalis 'Prostratus'	zone 8	Trailing rosemary

away, it helps to place the bar there, and use the drinks as a draw." But such movement must be planned as carefully as the garden itself.

Seats

Medieval garden seating was rustic and soft—that is, until the first chill of autumn. The seats were made of earth and turf, a simple bank at first, later confined by a wattle fence. Little meadow flowers and fragrant herbs such as chamomile often carpeted the turf. Later, the nineteenth-century garden offered seats of exquisite discomfort, modeled after gnarled trees.

Fortunately for you and your guests, these are two garden-seating ideas that have not proven timeless, while many of the earliest outdoor seating examples, such as the Italian Renaissance stone bench, remain unsurpassed in their simplicity, classic good sense, and appropriateness. Since it is widely agreed that every garden needs destinations, places for the eye—and the beholder—to rest, furniture does double duty. Thoughtful garden party-givers spend as much time choosing their outdoor furniture as they do selecting their plantings, and many feel it wise not to spare cost in doing so. Needless to say, such seating must harmonize with its surroundings and be used judiciously. In a small garden, too many permanent seats is visually jarring, as is ornate seating in a rustic garden.

Seating can either be movable or permanent. Furniture placed on a patio should be lightweight so that it can be moved around easily. Lawn furniture placed on grass, if weighty at all, should be given a foundation of bricks or tiles inserted into the grass under each foot. These not only level the seat and prevent damage to the grass, but they protect wooden legs from dampness and rot. Stone and weathered wood benches are permanent furniture and are often found tucked away, delightful retreats rewarding those who stroll down a path. There is something rare and wonderful about people sitting where they cannot be seen, enjoying secret places in the refreshing garden, occasionally happened upon by their fellow partygoers. Such seclusion could never be found in a living room. Handsome stone or reconstituted stone reproduc-

© Derek Fell

A garden with a gazebo is thrice blessed. This forever-magical structure provides seating, shade, and an irresistible destination point for a fern-lined pathway. As with any wooden structures, upkeep is essential.

tions of seventeenth- and eighteenth-century classic benches, carefully placed in settings deserving of them, give a garden a quality unmatched by any other addition. Such seating should not be placed on a lawn, which would suffer beneath it; grass would have to be clipped by hand around it, as well.

Garden furniture, of course, is subject to time and the elements, unless it is stored indoors. The softwoods commonly available will soon begin to rot if left outside unprotected. Woods with natural resistance are available, such as western red cedar, teak or iroko, though they may be more expensive. Whatever the wood, slatted benches allow rainwater to drain off, which is good for the seat as well as the sitter.

Screws used in garden furniture must be of brass or stainless steel. Even ordinary steel screws treated with protective lacquer or chromiumplated will rust, causing streaks and stains on the wood and weakening it as well. Such screws should be countersunk so they do not catch on clothing. Similarly, all glue used for outside furniture should be exterior-quality, or it will deteriorate.

Wooden garden furniture may be left natural or stained or painted, and wrought iron is traditionally painted black. Designers favor folding and deck chairs in neutral materials and patterns and avoid large floral prints. They are distracting and do not flatter those seated in them. The understated good taste generally found in interior design is the standard in today's gardens, since, as writer Dana Cowin put it in *HG* magazine, "The barriers separating the wild outdoors from the protected indoors are being broken down these days." Indeed, furniture from inside is even being taken out, and vice versa.

Weathered, peeling urns and statues are being cleaned up somewhat and invited inside, and garden furniture is often doing duty in the kitchen. Classic forms are being recast: Early American twig chairs in iron, rush in metal weave.

A number of traditional seats are now available for outdoor entertaining. Adirondack chairs, French cafe furniture, light-

© Courtesy of Crown Leisure Products

Classic forms in garden furniture are constantly being rethought, resulting in new
entertaining ideas, such as this Ironwood Mesh Lounge set—sturdy enough for comfort,
light enough to be moved where needed.

weight cast aluminum Victorian-style garden furniture, and the classic Lutyens bench updated with a waterproof finish and charming colors are now all possibilities for contemporary entertaining.

Creating seats can be fun, as well. Ordinary paving slabs offset by colorful plantings behind and to the side make an inexpensive bench, and can carry along the theme of the pathway. Wooden boards placed on ornate stone supports will eventually weather and come to resemble the stone itself. An old tree trunk placed on top of two stone supports creates a garden bench with a more rustic feel. Such permanent installations require a thoughtful appraisal of the view, the need for protection from the elements,

and exposure to the sun. Consider whether or not the ground nearby is level enough to support a table. The size of such a bench should not overwhelm the garden. A two-seater should be four to five feet (1.2 to 1.5 m) long, and seventeen to eighteen inches (42 to 45 cm) from the ground.

Teak has a high natural oil content, enabling it to resist rot and age to a rich silver-gray patina. Some environmentally concerned gardeners are questioning the use of teak for their outdoor furniture, since some supplies come from endangered rain forests. Most of it, in fact, is harvested and replanted on special plantations. If you have a concern about the source of a teak item, direct your questions to the store or manufacturer.

◄ In another example of a new thought on a classic design, wrought iron is formed into an old twig bench.

Lighting

The after-dark garden holds a special magic. At night, the garden has an aura of mystery, which can be enhanced with imaginative lighting design. Nature's own lighting is moonlight, and the luminous, dreamlike feeling it evokes is unsurpassable. Though the night's weather may be unpredictable, the moon appears as promised, offering her most glamorous effects from the half moon phase through five days after full moon. For two weeks during each month she is at her full power. Your local planetarium or the Farmer's Almanac will help you pinpoint the times of greatest moonglow. Many newspapers offer information about sunset and moonrise, as do meteorological services and calendars.

For times when moonlight is not enough, however, artificial lighting is a necessity. The graceful stone lantern is an integral part of Japanese garden design and, fortunately, many types and fashions of garden lighting are available today as well. Such lighting should always complement the tranquil nature of the nightscape and act as a gentle guide to the night garden's mysteries. Outdoor lighting can subtly augment moonlight to transform your night garden into a dream setting as well as a safe place to be.

Torches, hurricane lamps, and candles add effective touches. New Mexican Christmas revelers place small candles in sand-filled brown paper bags along walls and pathways, where they glimmer merrily—and safely—all evening. Called farolitas, these utilitarian decorations can line your driveway, be placed throughout the garden, or be added anywhere illumination is required. Though brown paper bags are an earthy touch, you might prefer the white candle bags available from some suppliers.

Landscape illumination specialists and landscape architects, rather than electricians, are valuable consultants for your creative garden-lighting requirements. Designers know how to divert insect-attracting lights from terraces and dining areas, and how

▲ The miracle of teak is that it looks better and better as it weathers, gaining a silvery sheen. Take care to make sure the source of your teak does not endanger the rainforest.

Courtesy of Liteform Designs

◄ New garden lighting fixtures are often inspired by the time-honored designs we fondly recognize. Here, an indisputably modern electric lantern proudly pays homage to its Japanese ancestor.

◄ ▼ How does your garden glow? Allow an expert to show you what under-lighting can do to dramatize your garden areas. Night lighting, to the garden host or hostess, is essential for the safety and enchantment of guests and should be very thoughtfully installed.

Courtesy of Nightscaping by Loran

best to conceal wiring. They often do this ingeniously, perhaps hiding the wires inside planters. Professionals use special filters to imitate the silvery moonlight or to flatter flesh tones. Warm, reddish lighting creates a sense of fun and excitement, while blue lighting sets a more subdued, romantic mood. The right lighting can even turn a weeping willow into a shimmering fountain of illumination. Tiny lights strung through trees are a popular night garden effect.

To determine the effect you will want your garden's lighting to have, observe how sunlight naturally falls on various spaces at different times of the day. Instead of duplicating the sun's designs, you may want your night garden to emphasize or mini-mize features in ways impossible in sunlight. Use shadow and reflection to cause such a transformation. Watch the effects of the moon, too.

No one should ever squint from too bright light, nor should you resort to the monotony of uniform lights stretching along a pathway. A little night magic can be achieved with low-voltage, glare-free lighting systems. Bright, white halogen footlights illu-minate trees dramatically. Post lights highlight walkways and entrance steps. For best results, garden lights are directed down-ward onto low foliage or beds of flowers, with large shades dis-persing the light to a wide area. Accent lights are used along walkways or stuck into foundation plantings, and can be placed at intervals along garden borders. If you are lighting your stairs, each step should be lit to avoid the "disappearance" of one, which could cause your guests to trip.

When mounted from above and aimed downward, floodlights provide spot lighting. When installed in the ground and directed upward, they highlight. Underwater pond lights will enliven an otherwise dark body of water and beautifully illuminate fish and lilies. Plants and steps are not all you will want to illuminate. Chimneys, gables, doors, columns, balustrades, and other architectural structures add dimension and integrate house and garden into the evening landscape.

Sound

You can change the mood of your garden and your party with the flick of a switch and the turn of the dial if your garden is wired for sound. We have entered the age of amazingly clear sound reproduction, thanks to the compact disc. You have probably become accustomed to the enhancing effects of beautiful music during all your indoor activities and in your car. You may even be one of the millions of people who orchestrate every activity in their lives with the help of a Walkman. You understand the positive effects and benefits of sound, so why not take them into the garden?

Imagine a Vivaldi-inspired garden walk, or a dalliance at dusk with Cole Porter. The soft, spirited sound of jazz, Pat Methany or Kenny G., carries you to the flowers and trees, and they almost seem to nod to the rhythm.

Harvey Steinberg and Mark Gantt of Linear Design have spent many years wiring outdoor spaces for sound. They have many caveats and cautions—along with a great deal of encouragement—to offer anyone considering supplying a garden with sound. The first caution concerns the temptation to do the job yourself or to have it done by a not-completely-qualified person. So many of Steinberg's assignments consist of straightening out work done by well-meaning amateurs that he unhesitatingly suggests homeowners hire an experienced audio contractor who can avoid the pitfalls and take advantage of the tremendous advances offered by the audio industry today.

The first thing a homeowner must do when considering an outdoor sound system is evaluate the yard or garden and its uses, present and future. What activities are you planning for the next year or two? Will family and guests be confined to one spot, or will some be playing badminton over there and others eating over

Though the sound of birds are often the most delightful music to be heard along a path such as this, there are times, perhaps during dinner, when "Nights in the Gardens of Spain," whispering from speakers placed along the path, would lift your garden gathering into a true party mode.

here? Where will you place dining tables? Most important, do you anticipate the addition of a deck, pool, or tennis court in the foreseeable future? It would be very expensive to rewire when your future swimming pool is finally dug and ready for sound. You will also regret having to disturb your lawn or garden and re-landscape a wiring installation later. If you plan ahead, extra lines meant to service areas not yet developed may be capped and brought to the surface of the garden, then topped off with a red flag so they are accessible for future use.

There are two ways of wiring for sound. Direct burial means just that: the laying in of wiring under the earth. Among other things, this method is vulnerable to digging mistakes by landscapers, which can interfere with the wiring and, therefore, with your system.

The second wiring method is the one our experts recommend. With this method, PVC plastic piping is laid in the ground with wiring threaded through it. This allows you to reach the wiring at any spot where it needs repair, since one or two nylon pull cords are generally installed inside the piping. The cord enables you to retrieve the wiring without bending it or digging up the piping.

Unforeseen things happen to wiring systems, so it is recommended that you always run more wire than you think you need; two lines more, Steinberg recommends. There is no appreciable difference in cost, except for the cost of the wire, as long as the laying of the additional lines is included in the initial wiring job. You will be glad you have added insurance in the long run.

Always run shielded wires, warns Steinberg. These resist radio and microwave output from neighbors. Wires can be shielded overall or individually shielded. If you are putting more than one type of signal out of a line—that is, multiple conductors off one cable, perhaps a CD player on one set of speakers, and a radio on another, with area amplifiers—you will want them to be individually shielded with a drain line.

Unless you have a heated cabana, for instance, all equipment except speakers should be kept inside the house, and never set up near a swimming pool. If you do use speakers sold through retail stores or through the mail, bring them inside in the dead of winter, Gantt recommends. This will lessen the chances of their not standing up to harsh conditions. Weatherized connections are important to use when speakers are the plug-in type. Your speakers, if they are touching the earth, should be grounded to ensure that lightning does not damage your system and the alternating current line.

As in many other industries, commercial audio products, though more expensive, offer more longevity for the money and are highly recommended. Many retail audio products, though advertised as "outdoor quality," may rot away in a few years. Commercial products are made to last. Their manufacturers, aware that contractors and professionals are their customers, make their equipment as problem-free and guaranteed as possible.

Commercial equipment is often modular, making it easier to add features or components, while non-professional, consumer-oriented equipment may not accept additional options. One feature, known as precedence effect, enables you to interrupt a musical program, for example, to tell someone in the garden that he or she has a phone call inside the house. Another feature enables you to listen to classical music inside the house, for instance, and light rock outside. The state-of-the-art reaches the commercial market well before it hits the audio stores, Steinberg says, so do not be confined by what you see on the market.

In deciding what kind of system you need, determine the level of ambient noise in your garden: What sounds are commonly heard at different times of day and night, and how loud are they? Is there a road or highway nearby, for instance? This is done with sound pressure level meter. Or go into your garden with a friend and hold a conversation at a normal vocal level. If you cannot be heard at a normal speaking level, your speakers will have to compensate, just as you do. This measurement is a good reference point for finding out how loud your music system has to be in order to be heard. Also consider your neighbors—both human and animal. You do not want your sound system to be so loud as to disturb those around you. If your house is fairly remote, and surrounded by a wildlife preserve, also be careful not to upset the natural balance.

The placement of speakers is an important decision. They must afford coverage, but not be so far from listeners that they will have to be blasted to be heard. Those nearest to such a speaker will find it uncomfortable, if not impossible to enjoy themselves. Some speakers will need to be individually adjusted higher and lower than others, as well.

Natural features of your property are likely to determine the

There is wire buried near this peaceful teatime scene, and two speakers are hidden nearby, but they do not interfere with the beauty of the setting. That is one of the secrets of good garden design: discretion. The other, say our experts at Linear Design, is safety.

placement of speakers. A rock formation or the side of the house may be a perfect spot, since the sound from speakers placed in the unbounded open air with nothing to reinforce it tends to get lost. Just the simple act of facing a speaker toward the house may serve to confine the sound in an effective way. Steinberg says that it is often wise to construct a wall simply to "flank" speaker noise.

The typical garden will use several small speakers, Steinberg says. They should be chosen for their sensitivity and efficiency and their dispersion characteristics. Some are meant to be buried flush with the ground; some are placed in trees and bushes, others mounted on the side of the house itself, making outside lines unnecessary.

It may be a surprise to hear that running a stereo system outdoors is senseless, but think about it. Unless you sit in one spot at all times and there is no ambient noise, those closest to one stereo speaker will hear only violins, and those listening to another speaker will hear only horns. This is one situation where old-fashioned mono is the best option.

An outside volume control resembling a dimmer switch is available, eliminating the need to run inside in order to raise or lower the sound in a garden. Infrared remote relay systems make it possible for you to regulate your sound or change radio stations without moving from your hammock.

Learning remotes have been developed that can be programmed to duplicate the functions of your various other remotes, grouping them together in one instrument. You also might find it useful to install a headphone jack with your volume controls. Steinberg's clients often request them for their Jacuzzis and other whirlpools.

The Audio Engineering Society and National Sound Engineers Association can recommend an audio contractor in your area. Some large contracting firms are listed in the Yellow Pages. Always find out the contractor's background and check references. Get a contract for what the professional services entail, price, time schedule, warranties, and future service calls. Not all people who call themselves contractors are qualified; happy clients are their best recommendation.

© Michael Skott

PART TWO

ADVICE FROM PROFESSIONALS AND PARTYGIVERS

There are, of course, as many styles of garden entertaining as there are gardens, hosts, and hostesses. There are also the garden additions that no living room requires: tents, for instance. There are sound and light setups, and sometimes caterers to deal with.

Here are interviews with people whose lives have been enriched because they have placed a welcome mat at the entrance to their gardens, and those who have worked for years at supplying the party garden with its needs. We thought it best to let these helpful advisors speak for themselves, to share the experiences that have taught them, year after year, how to make it as easy as possible to offer the garden to friends in a memorable, trouble-free way.

INTERVIEW

Partygivers Gill and Harry Patterson

Wherever you are on Gill and Harry Patterson's magical peninsula on New York's Shelter Island, you can see the water. Great blue herons are frequent guests, and they, too, are entertained by the discoveries that the Pattersons lovingly bring back to their private little peninsula from their six-months-of-the-year travels to India, Bali, Borneo, Sumatra, and other points east. "Gardens have to be shared," says Gill Patterson. "There's no joy in a garden that isn't."

The ankalon, a bamboo xylophone-type instrument from Indonesia that is used as a scarecrow there, is one of the delights that guests have come to expect in the Pattersons' garden. Then there is an entire "family" from Old Borneo, as well as Hepatongs, stately, anatomically correct grave figures, all carved out of tree trunks.

Treasures from India that have found a home in the garden include a palace bird feeder in the shape of a pagoda, which houses carved parrots, a seesaw with camel saddles, and a granite god of good fortune.

The Pattersons' parties are strictly geared to their garden, to its growing season, its peculiarities and its personality. It is an attractive garden from early spring to late autumn. By the end of June, there is an abundance of daylilies, and a party is always planned for mid-July to celebrate them, along with the different varieties of artemisia, phlox, matricaria, and shasta daisies. During the first week of October, the Montauk daisies and chrysanthemums are out. Twelve is a manageable number of guests for their parties, but the numbers vary.

Ground-length tablecloths and straw hats kept on hand for guests are among Gill Patterson's wise suggestions for summer outdoor partygiving.

© Michael Skott

Such is the climactic variability of the Patterson's garden area that forty feet (12 m) takes them to a different climate zone altogether. The Pattersons must consider each day's prevailing winds and heat. But always, the green-but-beachy resort feeling of this special island determines the food to be served.

"We love curries," says Gill Patterson. "Or big gumbos. Harry grills on the Weber Kettle outside and I'm usually busy with the rest of the meal inside." Outdoor entertaining usually means non-breakable service of a very good quality. "We are barefoot people," she says. "But our meals tend to be hot and saucy, so we always use rattan baskets under disposable plates to prevent accidents. And people tend to wander, as they should, during outdoor parties. It's not unusual to find an expensive wine glass on the beach the next day, so I find the best plastic glasses I can, and we use them."

Other considerations must be made when holding a party on Shelter Island. Deer ticks, which carry Lyme disease, are one. "I tell our guests to stay to our cut lawn areas, and we've mowed a path to the beach," Gill says. She fills tubes with cotton saturated with an anti-deer tick chemical, and places them every five yards (4.5 m) in the party area. She replaces the tubes twice a year.

As all successful garden partygivers do, the Pattersons give a great deal of thought to what will make their guests comfortable. They keep straw hats, hand fans, shawls and sweaters on hand at all times. They also stock up on sunblock, insect repellant, and citronella torches, which they place in the ground every six feet (2 m). Even their lawn is people-planned. Though it tends to attract bees, white clover is used as a ground cover because it is hardier than grass and is not harmed by foot traffic.

The Pattersons also try to make it easier on themselves. They make pre-party deadheading less of a chore by doing it with battery-operated clippers. They also keep a supply of eight card tables on hand, with folding plywood tabletops that accommodate eight. They rent folding chairs if they need them. There are always two cloths on every table. One is floor-length, so table legs do not show, covered with smaller cloths that handkerchief-point down. Colors and fabrics are mixed and matched to reinforce the feeling of casual entertaining.

The Patterson's guests are carefully mixed and matched too, and always with the warmth and thoughtful attention to detail that this host and hostess, no matter how far they travel, bring to their popular party garden at home.

INTERVIEW

Caterer Cynthia Atwood

Have you ever wondered how caterers keep salads looking fresh and beautifully designed even when the bowl is visited by guest after guest? Cynthia Atwood, who has assisted many a catered affair in the popular Berkshire Mountains area of Great Barrington, Massachusetts, says the secret is simple. "Don't refill when you can replace. As much as possible, make two of everything. Remove the half-emptied bowl or dish and slip the fresh one onto the table in its place."

Caterers are accustomed to using rented plates, which do not have to be thoroughly washed before their return to their rental company. But they do have to be rinsed, especially if they are kept where animals may be attracted to leftovers. Some caterers who cater outdoors have a quick method of dish-rinsing after the guests go home, one that any host or hostess might employ: the garden hose.

Atwood recommends that you count the rental dishes as soon as your caterer arrives. This way you'll avoid the caterer's worst nightmare: "You don't have enough dessert plates, so you have to wash the salad plates."

A no-no for catered outdoor dining? "Soup," Atwood says. "It's difficult to serve at the right temperature outdoors, and it's just too sloshy. And getting soup dishes all cleared away as people are about to go to the buffet is difficult, too."

INTERVIEW

Floral Designer Cheri Wagner

"A florist with a million ideas" is the definition of *florinaere,* according to Helmur Oliver, the ingenious Dutch woman who invented

the term. When Cheri Wagner first arrived in New York City from Virginia, she worked with the late Ms. Oliver, who not only

brought the idea of sophisticated florist shops to New York, but also invented the dying process that produced the black orchid.

When Ms. Oliver constructed a floral arrangement for her clients—many of whom were celebrities—she would sometimes throw it

across the room to make sure it held together. It was from her that Cheri Wagner learned techniques of the old school that, together

with her lifelong Southern garden party experience, make her the in-demand florinaere she is today.

The Southern garden parties of Wagner's childhood often lasted all day, she remembers, with a brunch evolving into an afternoon

poetry reading or musical recital, then gliding smoothly into dinner. "Elegance, rhythm, and charm" are the hallmarks of the

Southern garden party. "From the ladies' dresses to the hammock swinging, there is always that flow. Up north, garden parties

also have a great deal of style, in a more formal manner."

There are many delightful Southern flowers, trees, and customs Wagner has brought to her northern clients, and many more that

garden partygivers everywhere can adapt and use. Here are some:

▪ A catered party often means the absence of one element that will be missed: the grand aromas of good food in preparation. One way to compensate is to heat cinnamon sticks on the stove; the scent sets a celebratory mood to welcome the guests.

▪ Bring the inside out. Before you rent chairs, consider using your own rockers and other lighter chairs, and certainly wicker from the porch. If you have a bare wall, hang family portraits or old prints on it. If the wall is not attractive, drape it in fabric or mosquito netting, some of which is available now with subtle gold mesh. Is there a front porch swing? Have it placed in the garden —anything to enhance that swinging rhythm.

▪ Create natural party accessories culled from the garden, countryside, or seashore. Make napkin rings of willow stems and grape vines. Put a nice corsage pin through a lily pad leaf wrapped around a napkin. Take a big peony and small camellia, wire them together, and wrap a napkin around them. Clamshells make whimsical napkin holders. Napkins do not have to lie flat; they can emerge from a pot of flowers at each setting.

▪ Float edible flowers in the punch bowl, and put a small one in each drink. If you use stephanotis or jasmine, the scent will be wonderful as the glass is raised to the lips. Float flowers and candles on your pond or pool. Most flowers will float; simply cut them off close to the head.

▪ Instead of a tent, you can drape fabrics, such as netting, over poles or two-by-fours. Staple guns and stickum—a florist's putty that comes on a roll—are a great help with this.

▪ Florist's wire comes in rolls in different gauges. Use it to wire pinecones together, to make corsages, wreaths, and countless other things. Using wire, you can attach streamers, so that they flow from a bow or attach ivies so that they flow out of baskets.

▪ It is a joy to combine flowers with fruit, to create a still life on the table that looks as if it grew there. Place ivy among grapevines; contrast plants, flowers, and objects of shocking colors with grapes, rambling roses, and other plantings. Use a hollowed out squash, or a melon in lieu of a vase for flowers.

▪ Match nature's moods. When using flowers that are lacy, such as lilacs, complement them with lacy tablecloths.

Don't be afraid to enhance your floral arrangements with unusual ingredients. Sometimes an odd piece, such as this fish, can be just the thing to draw out a color in the flowers or integrate the individual offerings of the garden.

▪ Use vases for candles, too. You get a dramatic effect with several very tall dripless candles standing in a tall vase on a stone bench. Make a grouping of the candles, as you would flowers.

▪ Men love boutonnieres. Put a peacock feather behind a bachelor button. Wagner uses old crow feathers for bourbon drinkers, miniature seahorses for men's lapels, and silk ribbons with swallowtail points on the bottom.

▪ Decorate table umbrellas with flowers and ribbons cascading from the top, attached at each ribbed point, or perhaps hanging down from the inside. Do not let the decorations get in the way of people moving in to sit down; they should hang down only as far as to the table. Also try gathering the tablecloth at the sides of the table with a rubber band, which will not be seen once you insert flowers through it.

▪ Be playful with your garden party invitations too. Add something like a sprig of baby's breath or dried flowers, or even pressed or paper violets. Use flower stickers to seal envelopes.

▪ Use lovely old picture frames to indicate table numbers and place names for larger, more formal parties.

▪ To really give the party a garden feel, add two or three drops of rose water or orange blossom water to the bottom of a champagne glass. No more, though, or it will taste like soap!

INTERVIEW

Tent Supplier Gardner W. Hubbard

Gardner Hubbard puts up several hundred tents a year throughout Connecticut, and as many as sixty on a busy weekend.

A traditional Yankee who takes pride in his work, Hubbard took over his father's New Haven company, Cunningham and Upson, Inc.

in 1971. The company has enjoyed a fine reputation since 1854.

Hubbard has strong opinions on tent color. "White tents are all the rage for weddings right now. Well, I don't have any

white tents. Usually they're vinyl, or else they would be very difficult to keep clean, so they cost ten to fifteen percent more.

And I prefer canvas. Wait and see, white will go out of style. Sometimes when a bride wants white I say,

'How about a nice pink and white?' and her eyes light up."

Based on Hubbard's experience, here are some things to consider when planning a party in a tent:

It is far better if a representative of the tent company visits the site, since clients cannot always correctly measure their party spaces.

Also, the tent supplier needs to make sure that the ground is level at the party site.

One party coordinator always makes a graph of the yard or garden, showing where the tent should be placed in relation to everything

else. Be aware that tents can be of different sizes and shapes, because they are laced together modularly. With the help of

a tent expert, you may find creative designs possible.

▶▶ A clean, well-constructed tent brings the outdoors in, and colorful tablecloths create a garden of another kind. For a sitdown dinner such as this set up by Mary Cleaver, allow ten to twelve square feet (1 to 2 sq m) of tent per person, advises Gardner Hubbard.

▶ Florists can be called upon to decorate the insides of tents, though you must be careful in your choice of flowers, as it gets hot up there. Here, New York caterer Mary Cleaver used evergreen swags and little twinkling lights to camouflage the inside structure of the tent without wilting. Remember to have the florist remove the decorations before the tent is broken down.

■ Frame tents can easily be placed over swimming pools, patios, and decks. This type of tent is also called a "fiesta" and is held up with a metal frame and no center pole; a pole tent is what we think of as a "circus tent," because it has the traditional stakes, guideline ropes, and metal pipes to hold it up.

■ Florists often decorate the stakes, cords, and pipes of pole tents with pine branches and flowers. Have the florist return to the site, before the tent people come to "break down," to undo the flowers for you.

■ A sitdown dinner requires ten or twelve square feet (.9 to 2 sq m) of tent per person, including tables and chairs. For a cocktail party, figure on six square feet (.5 sq m). Also allow space for the band, bar(s), and food areas, as well as open areas for people to mingle.

■ Tents are heated in winter with heaters that have individual generators, so you will not risk an energy drain.

■ The use of drop cloths when tents are being erected is important to keep a tent spotless. Chances are you may not be able to see a tent company's wares in the air before you choose a company, but you can make it clear that you want a clean tent. Hubbard's tents are downgraded as they begin to show wear and tear, he says, with the oldest going to commercial work.

■ Do-it-yourself tents are available from some rent-all places, but they are often not structurally sound, with flimsy metal poles.

■ Tents should be grounded if there is the possibility of a lightning storm occuring in your area.

■ Hubbard always provides the tent sides, but sometimes leaves them on the premises in a bag, as they are easily hooked over the tent cord if needed.

■ It is not wise to cook with open flame in a tent.

If you keep these considerations in mind, selecting the perfect tent for your party should be an easy task.

© Michael Skott

INTERVIEW

Partygiver Sharyn Grossman

The outdoor parties Sharyn Grossman holds at her home in Amagansett, Long Island, New York, are famous for two things: the exquisite planning that goes into them and their warm, relaxed atmosphere. It is clear that the first leads to the second.

"I would never give a party that does not have a theme," she says. "People love it when the food, the design, and what people wear are all related. One of my favorite recent garden parties was given by a woman who served all these magnificent breads. She cut them up, arranged them prettily—with great style in baskets—accompanied by creamery herb butter in crocks. That was the first course, and it is what I remember most."

Grossman points out that the theme should extend beyond the food you serve. "Color and form are very important, especially outside, where there are no painted walls to restrict you. You are freer to create. I bring people out into the garden as soon as I can in spring, and keep them there as late as I can in fall. An autumn theme calls for decorating with leaves, for instance, which you can do beautifully outside."

She also has some helpful advice on making guests feel at home.

"The trick is to make each guest feel as if his or her arrival is the best thing to happen all day. Special attention at the door will help."

Grossman is sure to have party favors at the door for arriving guests.

Fill containers with your favorite blooming flowers, Grossman suggests, and place them all around your garden.

Among other useful tips from Grossman are the following:

■ Buy flats of your favorite plantings, remove them from their plastic holders, and place them in a pretty bowl with a bit of water. You will not have wasted any money, since you will plant them after the party is over.

■ Offer dieters fruit desserts.

■ Do not be afraid to serve messy desserts outdoors, since entertaining rules are relaxed at garden parties.

■ Mix good serving bowls and silver serving pieces with casual tableware.

■ Acquire a collection of reasonably priced but high-quality items from flea markets and yard sales.

■ Be prepared to move the party indoors, in the event of rain. Put wet umbrellas in the bathtub.

■ Adding vanilla, almond, chocolate, or cinnamon to coffee is a nice touch at garden parties. Also have a selection of special teas on hand.

As a final bit of advice, Grossman says, "I can't overemphasize the importance of planning for a garden party. When to serve the hors d'oeuvres, how long that will take, when to serve the main meal, which can't be brought out too soon or the party will be over too soon. Decide when the main meal is going to be cleaned off, and when you'll serve dessert. All this has to be scheduled and carefully coordinated, keeping in mind that the average party runs for four or five hours.

"Planning means you'll be free to visit with guests and enjoy yourself. It means nobody will drink too much, and there will be enough food. It means the party will end when it should."

INTERVIEW

Maitre D' Jon Imparato

Jon Imparato's New York City garden was once shaded by an enormous tree. One bolt of lightning later, the tree was felled, letting

the sunlight in that would transform—with Imparato's help—a bare brown square into the lush, exquisite retreat that he and his friends

and clients call "mecca." Jon not only caters small dinner parties for selected clients in his garden, he is also a highly experienced

captain and maitre d' who troubleshoots and facilitates large and small garden parties alike for his New York area clients.

The pleasures of garden entertaining are great, he agrees, and a few extra planning steps on the part of the party host can

make the gathering an even greater success.

Work begins with a staff meeting on the grounds before a party, says Imparato, and he encourages the client to be present to

introduce him- or herself. "The way a catering employee is treated will determine whether he or she will say 'No' when a guest asks

for apple juice, or, instead, will look for the juice in the refrigerator," says Jon.

It is very important for clients to be organized before the caterer comes, Jon emphasizes. Be sure, when you interview caterers,

that you and the caterer agree on where the vast amounts of rental equipment, kitchen appliances, bar furnishings, and so on, are to

be placed. Parties get off to a shaky start when equipment is shifted from place to place by the waiters who should be spending their

energy graciously serving the meal. The party location should be visited first, of course, and the aesthetics of the occasion must be considered. Have some idea of what you want so you are one step ahead of the caterer, but listen to his or her ideas, too.

Also be sure that your waste-disposal area is well out of the way of guests. For one thing, it is noisy there and always unattractive. Homeowners often get upset at finding the sanitation areas they have chosen before the party are not really the best areas at party time. If no alternative places have been prepared, problems develop. If the area you choose cannot be concealed, rent screens.

Imparato also has caveats on serving the food. He advises that you do not pre-place hors d'oeuvres before the main meal begins, though it is a practice often urged by caterers, since it saves them time. Before the party the sides of tents are sometimes covered in plastic and the sun beats down on them. The plastic is lifted up as the party is about to begin, but the food has already gotten unpleasantly warm. Putting food out closer to the serving time makes less of a gathering place for bugs, also makes the food better and more appetizing.

Seventy-five guests or fewer can be comfortably served at an outdoor sit-down dinner. For more, a buffet is recommended.

If you are having a sit-down dinner, do not request butler service—which means a platter is brought around and guests serve themselves—unless you are sure your guests know how to handle it gracefully. Otherwise, request French service, which means food is served from a tray, or have food brought out on plates. Seventy-five people is the limit for the number of people comfortably served at a sit-down dinner, according to Imparato's experience; for more than that a buffet is in order.

One of the reasons that clients may resist the idea of a buffet, even though it is usually more practical than a sit-down dinner, is because they think guests will all flock to the buffet table at once. Imparato says a simple solution is to ask guests to approach the buffet table by table. People eat a lot more at a buffet, and food is kept very hot with Sterno.

In dealing with a caterer, remember that it is your party, your expense, and your food choices. If a caterer suggests a certain hors d'oeuvres, it may be because it is easy to serve or he or she is using that food item for several parties that weekend. If you are happy with the suggestion, do not worry about it. If you are not, feel free to ask for alternatives. Salmon and ratatouille in pastry shells are good examples of popular, handheld hors d'oeuvres, for an outdoor party at which guests are standing during the first course. Because food often sits in the baking sun, he does not recommend serving sushi at an outdoor, afternoon party.

Very often clients think a valet parking service is unnecessary, but a bad parking situation could leave guests walking on country roads in party shoes. Caterers can usually supply valet personnel at a reasonable cost, says Jon. Other important points to keep in mind are the following:

■ Taking inventory of electrical outlets is an important pre-party consideration. Large coffeemakers take a lot of voltage. Three big pots on the same line can overload the circuit breakers. Imparato recommends placing one or two coffee and hot water makers elsewhere, even in the basement or the garage. The coffee will be poured into a samovar to be served, anyway, and kept hot with Sterno.

■ Candles near tents are another danger. Imparato emphasizes taking great caution about the placement of candles in general. Remember that grass and weeds ignite easily.

■ Be sure to ask for photographs of the food presentations promised by a caterer you do not know, he says. Know your rights in this regard. Someone's description may not turn out to be what you expected.

■ The cocktail hour should be just that—one hour long. Limiting the cocktail period prevents guests from tiring out early, and some chairs and small tables should always be provided.

■ Hiring a "CJ," or compact disc jockey, will not only save you money, but also create a more pleasant atmosphere. A disc jockey can play the real Glenn Miller, with guaranteed rhythm every time. The caterer can help you find a "CJ." A harpist or a chamber group can also be hired—your local college can usually suggest one—for the cocktail hour.

■ Always know where the rental equipment and garbage should be put at the end of the party so you don't have to bother with the problem. And always ensure that the caterer leaves the kitchen in the condition it was found.

■ Have the following on hand before a catered party: heavy-duty garbage bags, milk and half-and-half, sweetener and sugar, paper towels, and cleaning fluids. Caterers sometimes forget or do not have enough of these essential items.

■ Never think you can buy too much ice. Waiters alone, especially in summer, can use five pounds of ice for their own water glasses.

■ Garages employed for setup or preparation of food must be cleaned up. Rakes could fall on waiters' heads, tools could be stepped on. Put it all in a corner, with a piece of canvas over it, or secured elsewhere, and leave nothing hanging down from above.

■ Wine, sparkling water, juices, and champagne are currently favored for cocktail hours and parties; hard liquor is less in favor.

■ To be certain that tips are received by the party servers and waiters, put them in labelled envelopes and have someone hand the envelopes to each one. A before-party promise of tips will, of

Champagne is among the honored guests at the cocktail hour, which should last no longer than sixty minutes, says caterer Mary Cleaver.

course, ensure grateful service from a hard-working staff.

■ Allow catering staff to wear white shirts and black vests in place of the weighty tuxedo jackets on a hot summer day. An uncomfortable staff means poorer service.

■ At catered parties the staff may go without food if the party-giver does not allow for the extra meals. If you want sparkling personalities and even tempers, decent food for the staff is one way to ensure it.

■ Do not think you are saving money by entertaining fifty guests instead of one hundred. The expense will be so close in numbers that it might be wise to invite more.

Imparato greatly prefers garden parties held in the daytime. Even in summer there is the risk of a nighttime chill, he says, and the dangers—particularly if women are wearing high heels—are not to be underestimated.

■ The best parties proceed flawlessly if caterers, their staffs, and the partygiver work as partners, says Imparato. Everyone must think ahead.

© Charles Mann

Partygivers Scott Markman and Toshi Kawahara

Scott Markman and Toshi Kawahara could build an entertaining garden on the moon. They are creating one right now out of a twenty-acre sea of mud surrounding their house in Abiquiu, New Mexico—Georgia O'Keefe's old neighborhood outside of Santa Fe. They moved here after ten years of living in Los Angeles and entertaining in their exquisite garden, which they designed and maintained.

To have a garden and not entertain in it is unthinkable to Markman, who has been a landscaper for fifteen years. "People feel freer and more relaxed in the garden, because they don't have the constraints of the walls and the ceilings. Instead, there's sky, sun, birds and crickets." The trick, Markman and Kawahara have found, is to allow your entertaining to be as spontaneous as the nature around you, as easily flowing as a waterfall.

When do they entertain? "When something is in bloom," is Kawahara's easy answer. It is a Japanese answer, but it is one Markman would also give, because their attitudes easily bridge east and west. "In Los Angeles we would regularly have people over simply because the garden looked so beautiful. For four we plan a sitdown dinner, for more we have a buffet. In Los Angeles we'd put down a really nice rug and pillows on the lawn, with some chairs for those who'd rather sit," he says.

Now that they have relocated, there inevitably will be changes in their garden-party agenda. Los Angeles gardens are welcoming virtually all year 'round, except in August's smog and February's rain. In Santa Fe, they look forward to inviting people to the garden in

The Southwest's prickly pear cactus is an excellent example of a plant that, though beautiful, should be viewed from afar and not planted near seating for guests. The Meteor Shower party described on page 110 calls for exotic, offbeat plants such as this.

© Charles Mann

winter—to take them from there, bundled up, for walks on their twenty acres. They will have a fire pit where their guests will bake potatoes and roast marshmallows, and they will have an outdoor sauna.

They are designing their Southwestern garden so that it will be home to their meadowlarks and magpies, with native plants and an area of roses and peonies, as well as irises, wildflowers, and a lawn. The garden will lead directly into an orchard, whose trees are only three or four feet (90 cm to 120 cm) tall now. They have planted a twelve-foot (4-m) willow, and will plant a few more trees, because shade is vital during New Mexican summers. They will definitely revive their custom of eating on the ground, and so have packed away their dhurries and Indian blankets. They have also planned a great deal of seating for the garden itself. "The sun hits the garden in different places at different times," says Kawahara, "so your seating should follow the warmth."

As garden professionals and successful garden partygivers, Markman and Kawahara have solid advice for those who would like to entertain as comfortably outdoors as they do indoors.

■ Plan, plan, plan. "My landscaping clients sometimes know they will have a party in two weeks, but they don't tell me until a week before the party, and it really doesn't work," says Kawahara, "because in two weeks the plants are still very small. Start planting a month ahead for a party. Don't just put things in so it looks like a shopping center."

■ Understand your garden. Know what blooms when and how long it takes. "Go to your garden often to find out what's going on," suggests Kawahara. "Don't just look at it from the window."

■ Deadhead and prune a week before. But rake the leaves the morning of the party, just as you would dust your house. Water one or two days before so the area will be refreshed, though largely dry.

■ Your "hardscape"—paths and patios—should be very accessible, designed to lead people from the house to outside. Have paths designed to entice people into hidden corners of the garden.

■ Some plants are friendlier than others, and should be invited to your garden parties. Friendly plants have deep green leaves, and are rounder than they are spiky. Cactus or thorny plants near seats are forbidding, as are plantings that attract bees. Even overwhelming scents, such as jasmine, can be annoying to guests. Azalea is a very friendly plant, comments Markman. Kawahara also suggests examining the height of a plant in relation to where people will be seated. It is not comfortable to be dwarfed by a large plant or something gangly, or even a planting that is too small.

■ Steer guests away from your soil; stepping on it deprives plants of nitrogen, which they take from the air. This is a very good argument for accessible paths.

■ As much as possible, use your own flowers for the table. Little pots of homegrown tulips, cyclamen, and freesia are one suggestion.

Markman provides an additional strong argument for garden entertaining: "All that light, color, those smells and textures are things we can't possibly have in our houses, though we try to imitate them. The garden is the source of all that joy and beauty. What a pleasure to share it with people we love."

You will not find the typical autumn display of colorful leaves in New Mexico, but instead, Markman and Kawahara enjoy exposing their East Coast friends to the Southwest's distinctive offerings. The change of seasons there brings charming blooms to purple aster and chamisa.

PART THREE

THE GARDEN PARTIES

© Michael Skott

The descriptions of theme parties that follow are meant as guides, as jumping-off points for your own creativity. Expect one idea to lead to another, and you will come up with unique approaches that we could not have imagined.

The important thing, as Sharyn Grossman puts it, is to "take a theme and run with it. Carry it out to its farthest conclusion. When you think you've come to the end of your ideas, expect more." As most of our advisors agree, the key to even the most casual gathering is planning—not last-minute planning, but the thoughtful, early immersion into an idea that makes last-minute spontaneity possible.

Whatever motif you choose as a reason for holding a party in your garden, the central theme should never change: a flowing party with an easy grace, leaving memories as bright as blossoms.

APR

Step-Into-Spring
Luncheon

for Eight

Asparagus Timbales

*Baked Free-Range Chickens with Sage and
Salt Dough Crust*

Fiddlehead Fern Sauté

Strawberry Tart with White Chocolate Sauce

Here is a light-hearted party to welcome the earliest flowers of the season and the first warmth that invites them into your garden. The flowers themselves will lend their color schemes to your decorations, so expect this gathering to be alive with reds, yellows, and purples. There should be pots of proud, colorful tulips and other early flowers everywhere. Parade their fragrances freely today—it has been a long and dormant winter.

Surprises such as tiny speckled specialty candies that resemble newly hatched birds' eggs would be charming in small bright baskets. If they are small enough, the baskets might be used as place markers and party favors.

This would be a wonderful time to fill Victorian bird cages with flowers. Or take an example from the Eastern Europeans, who step into spring by baking tasty braided breads that embrace painted eggs. Take an inventory of your new buds and watch how the number increases day to day. Make dandelion wine, pick fiddlehead ferns.

Fiddlehead ferns are shoots from the ostrich fern. Their taste is similar to both that of asparagus and artichokes. Regardless of which one of these vegetables they most resemble, they are unmistakably delicious. Recently they seem to have permeated

the world of unusual culinary finds. Perhaps their short season of about a month in early spring has something to do with their popularity. They are wonderful when sautéed in good olive oil and garlic. Be careful not to overcook since their natural crispy flavor should not be sacrificed to too much contact with the heat.

What a perfect occasion for window boxes abloom with lilies of the valley and for a stunning centerpiece of white lilacs surrounded with crabapple, dogwood, and forsythia branches.

Birds and butterflies will be among your cheerful guests today. Do some research because you will be asked "Whose song is that?," "Is that a monarch?," and "What is over there that the hummingbirds love so much?"

The most natural music for this gathering will be coming from the trees and the delighted conversation of the guests. But it might also be a time for a little light and joyful Vivaldi.

© Steven Mark Needham/Envision

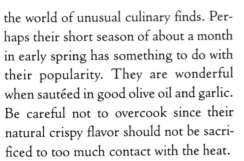

© Robert Lima/Envision

ASPARAGUS TIMBALES

3/4 cup heavy cream

1 cup chicken broth

5 eggs

3/4 teaspoon salt

1/2 teaspoon ground white pepper

Pinch of nutmeg

1 1/2 cups cooked, finely chopped asparagus

1/2 cup grated Parmesan cheese

Preheat oven to 350 degrees F. In a large mixing bowl, combine cream, broth, eggs, salt, pepper, and nutmeg. Beat well with a wire whisk. Add asparagus and cheese. Mix to blend well.

Butter eight 2-inch ceramic, glass, or disposable tinfoil timbale molds. Pour enough custard into each mold to come within 1/4-inch of the tops. Line the molds up in a 2-inch-deep ovenproof baking pan large enough to hold the molds in one layer. Fill the pan with enough boiling water to come just beneath the tops of the molds. Cover them with a sheet of buttered parchment or wax paper.

Bake in the middle of the oven for 35 to 45 minutes or until a toothpick inserted in center of timbales comes out clean. Serve with toasted French bread croustades.

BAKED FREE-RANGE CHICKENS WITH SAGE AND SALT DOUGH CRUST

Two 3 1/2- to 4-pound chickens

2 to 4 bunches fresh sage leaves, plus extra sprigs for garnish

30 cloves garlic

Ground white pepper

4 cups all-purpose flour

4 cups kosher salt

Preheat oven to 425 degrees F. Wash the chickens under cold water. Pat dry with paper towels inside and out. Carefully loosen the skin from the flesh of the birds and insert 3 to 4 leaves of sage on the breast under the skin. Fill the cavities of the birds with equal amounts of whole garlic cloves, white pepper, and remaining sage leaves.

In a large mixing bowl, combine flour and salt. Add enough cold water to make a spreadable paste. Divide evenly between the two birds and spread the dough to completely cover each chicken. They should be completely encased in the dough so no parts of the chickens are left showing.

Bake in oven for 45 minutes, or until dough is golden brown. Remove from oven and allow chickens to rest for 10 minutes. The crust will be extremely hard and may require a sharp knife to cut the crust away from the chickens. Remove the crust and discard. Serve whole chickens on beds of fresh sage leaves.

FIDDLEHEAD FERN SAUTÉ

3 tablespoons extra virgin olive oil
1 tablespoon butter
2 to 3 large cloves garlic, crushed
1¹/₂ pounds fiddleheads
Salt and pepper, to taste

In a 12-inch skillet, heat oil and butter over high heat. When butter has melted and starts to brown slightly, add garlic. Cook, stirring constantly, 30 seconds. Add fiddleheads. Cook, stirring constantly, 2 to 3 minutes. Season with salt and pepper and remove from heat. Serve immediately.

SPRING-FLOWERING BULBS

You must plan in advance if you want your spring garden to feature the lovely flowers of bulbs. Most of them need to be planted in the fall. Here is a list of our favorites:

Daffodils

Narcissus minor minimus	zone 4	Narcissus
Narcissus triandus albus	zone 4	Angel's tears
Narcissus poeticus	zone 4	Poet's daffodil

Tulips

Tulipa x *hybrida* 'Darwinii'	zone 4	Darwin hybrid tulips
Tulipa primulina	zone 4	Primrose tulip
Tulipa kaufmanniana	zone 4	Waterlily tulip

Hyacinths

Hyacinthus orientalis	zone 6	Common hyacinth
Camassia scilloides	zone 5	Wild hyacinth
Muscari armeniacum	zone 4	Grape hyacinth

MAY

Derby Day Cocktail Party
for Twenty

Marinated Swordfish Kebobs
Black-Eyed Pea Relish
Stuffed Chicken Legs with Black Pepper Pâté
Angels and Devils on Horseback
Mint Juleps

In Kentucky, America's Derby capital, they arrive from Churchill Downs the first Saturday in May to dance on verandas among the pink and white dogwoods on Derby Day. Bars are set up on screened porches and patios. Neighborhood friends or party staff carrying hors d'oeuvre trays wear the caps and sometimes the silks of Derby jockeys, silks that may very well match the tablecloths. Laughter and bright colors dance in the breeze.

The Derby theme is all-encompassing, yet it is the details that seem to be remembered most from year to year. Horseshoes are decorated with red roses in honor of "The Run for the Roses"

that inspires these galas, and there may even be a live pony tethered to a tree outside. There are horseshoe-shaped cakes and jazz, and stone planters containing handsome horses' heads sculpted in ice, surrounded by hundreds of oysters in ice cubes.

Basic fare such as ham, turkey, beef, cheeses, and other standards are not considered boring on Derby Day, but rather traditional, familiar, and welcome, though menus vary as far as a horse can dash. Marinated Swordfish Kebobs, Stuffed Chicken Legs with Black Pepper Pâté, Black-eyed Pea Relish, and aptly named Angels and Devils on Horseback are cocktail fare today, all

---

84

augmented by the classic Mint Julep.

Derby hosts and hostesses are experts on keeping their parties mobile. Not passing too many drinks on trays is one secret, since guests who have to cross the yard for a drink will mingle. Hosts and hostesses also deliberately provide fewer chairs than there are guests, guaranteeing movement and flow.

Louisville Derby Day partygoers who are seated will sometimes blow a penny-whistle when they want another drink, or when the Belle of Louisville goes by. Though you may not have a paddle-wheeler to salute, you can promote a lot of fun with whistle-blowing.

Since Derby Day always enjoys warm weather, transparent tents are sometimes rented, so guests can enjoy an outdoorsy, country feel and be sheltered as well. Topiary horses are likely to run through the scene and sometimes act as center-pieces, whether the party is held on a patio or in an open field or a house. Pegasus—sometimes flying from among the calla lilies on a centerpiece pole—is a perennial Derby Day guest.

Invitations are carefully designed and planned each year. Some may be hand delivered, accompanied by a long-stemmed rose. Another invitation idea is a foldout of an old-fashioned garden with flowers, lace, and Japanese lanterns.

Derby Day means sprays of white tulips and roses nested in greenery on tables, ascots on men and hats on ladies —big, bold, unabashedly beautiful hats that set an unmistakable tone. Derby Day also means a trumpet announcing the start of the televised race, and two crossed bottles of champagne in a silver bucket to celebrate the winner. It means gifts for each guest, perhaps the Kentucky classic Makers Mark Bourbon, or a set of Derby glasses in a special box.

Racing memorabilia can be gathered from all over for your Derby Day: Not only Kentucky, but Ascot, Saratoga, and Belmont can lend their flavors. A little research will go a long way. Borrow riding paraphernalia, a crop for the wall, a blanket for over a chair, and a saddle to straddle a fence or a bar, as if they were not props at all, but the casual remnants of a morning spent astride a dashing mount, planning a cocktail afternoon for your favorite applauding, appreciative fans.

MARINATED SWORDFISH KEBOBS

$1/2$ cup honey

$1/3$ cup dark soy sauce

$1/2$ cup dry sherry

2 tablespoons hot red pepper flakes

$1/2$ cup champagne vinegar

1 cup safflower oil

8 pounds swordfish steaks, cut into 1-inch cubes

In a large mixing bowl, combine honey, soy sauce, sherry, red pepper flakes, vinegar, and oil. Add swordfish. Toss to coat and marinate 25 to 30 minutes. Preheat broiler. Skewer swordfish onto 20 skewers. Broil 8 to 10 minutes, or until golden brown and fish flakes easily, turning kebobs frequently and brushing with marinade.

BLACK-EYED PEA RELISH

2 cups dried or 4 cups canned black-eyed peas

2 cups chopped celery

1 cup minced onion

2 cups diced red bell pepper

2 large cloves garlic

1 whole small jalapeño pepper

2 tablespoons sugar

1 cup dairy sour cream

2 tablespoons balsamic vinegar

1 tablespoon salt

1 to 2 tablespoons chopped fresh oregano or $1/2$ to 1 teaspoon dried

$1/2$ cup chopped fresh parsley

If using dried peas, place peas in a large, deep pot. Add enough water to cover peas by 2 inches. Let them soak overnight or at least 6 to 8 hours.

Drain. Cover with enough fresh, cold water to cover by 2 inches. Bring to boil over high heat. Skim the surface foam. Reduce heat to medium, cover and simmer about 1 hour or until tender. When cooked, drain and cool completely.

In a large mixing bowl, combine celery, onion, red pepper, and cooled peas. Toss well. In the bowl of a food processor combine garlic, jalapeño, sugar, sour cream, vinegar, salt, and oregano. Blend well until all ingredients are finely chopped. Combine dressing with peas. Sprinkle with chopped parsley and toss well. Chill overnight.

ANGELS ON HORSEBACK

¹/₄ cup vegetable oil

16 slices white bread, cut into rounds using canape cutter

16 shucked oysters

8 thin slices of prosciutto ham, cut in half (can substitute bacon)

Preheat oven to 400 degrees F. In a 12-inch skillet, heat oil over medium-high heat. When hot, add bread rounds and cook 30 to 60 seconds on each side or until golden. Drain on paper towels and reserve. In a small ovenproof dish large enough to hold angels, wrap large drained oysters with prosciutto. Secure each with toothpicks and bake about 3 minutes, or until ham is lightly browned. Drain well, remove picks and serve on toasts.

DEVILS ON HORSEBACK

Follow the same procedure as above substituting dried prunes for oysters and bacon for prosciutto.

MINT JULEPS

5 cups water

10 cups sugar

4 cups fresh mint leaves, plus extra sprigs for garnish

Shaved ice

1 liter bourbon

In a 2-quart saucepan, combine water, sugar, and mint leaves. Bring to boil over high heat, stirring until sugar has completely dissolved. Cook for 5 minutes or until sugar-water mixture is slightly syrupy (not longer than 8 minutes). Strain the syrup into a pitcher and chill thoroughly.

For each julep, place 2 tablespoons chilled syrup and about one half dozen mint leaves in the bottom of a tall glass or traditional mint julep cup. Mash the leaves in the syrup with the back of a spoon. Fill the glass with shaved ice tightly packed. Pour in 1 to 2 ounces bourbon. Fill the remaining spare space with the remaining mint syrup. Garnish with a fresh mint sprig.

© Rudy Muller/Envision

DERBY DAY GARDEN DECOR

The following trees and plants are integral to a Derby Day celebration, no matter which race you are honoring, the Kentucky Derby, Ascot in Great Britain, or the Triple Crown on Long Island in New York.

Salix alba 'Tristis' zone 2 Golden Weeping Willow

Lucky is the person whose garden contains a weeping willow, with graceful boughs bending toward the ground. 'Tristis' is one of the hardiest varieties, and a good selection for planting in moist soil.

Salix discolor zone 2 Pussy Willow

A hardy, but not particularly beautiful shrub, though valued for its soft catkins.

Gardenia jasminoides zone 8–9 Gardenia

Unless you live south of zone 7, you may have some trouble growing gardenias. If you cannot grow them you will want to buy them from a florist to decorate your Derby Day tables.

Jasminum nudiflorum zone 5 Winter Jasmine

This is another lovely flower for table decorations or boutonnières for your guests. This is the hardiest of all the jasmine, but it blooms early in April so you may need to buy it from your florist for a May celebration.

Grandiflora rose Queen Elizabeth

The lovely pink Queen Elizabeth rose seems appropriate for Ascot festivities. This is the highest rated and one of the most popular grandiflora roses.

Pelargonium x *horotum* zone 10 Geranium

Geraniums should decorate the table of a Triple Crown celebration. This species is the most common, but there are many lovely and unusual alternatives. Explore the scented geraniums, such as *P.* x *limoneum* (lemon) or *P. odoratissimum* (nutmeg).

© Bo Parker

MAY

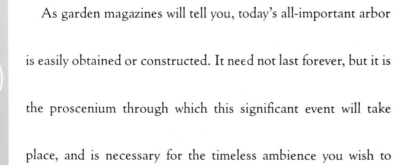

Arbor Wedding

for Fifty

*Broiled Jumbo Prawns with Hot
Mustard-Mango Sauce

*Miniature Layered Vegetable Pastries

Crudites Baskets

Cherry Tomatoes Stuffed with Crabmeat

*Honey-and-Grain Mustard Marinated
Cornish Game Hens

*Seared Tuna Salad

Haricot Verts

Shoestring Pomme Frites

Apricot and Almond Wedding Cake*

Ideally, your garden will dictate the color scheme of your wedding. This is where photographs taken the year before and careful notes about what has been planted since will come in handy. This is, of course, a time for the splendor of the rose to take second place only to the bride.

As garden magazines will tell you, today's all-important arbor is easily obtained or constructed. It need not last forever, but it is the proscenium through which this significant event will take place, and is necessary for the timeless ambience you wish to create. Every wedding needs an aisle, and you can create a lovely white one with attractive white material.

Of course, the arbor wedding is a classic sit-down dinner, complete with place cards to carefully ensure that out-of-town relatives get to talk to the in-towners, and that the attractive brother of the bride may enjoy the company of the groom's shy cousin. You will want to be in complete control of the flow of action, directing waiters to offer Kir Royales as guests stroll from the receiving line, for instance.

With your garden lending its abundant color to the setting, white is for your rented chairs, as well as for the tablecloths and napkins. If there is to be a tent, consider white only if you are certain it will be spotlessly clean and put up far enough in advance to ensure that. If not, pink or yellow is a lovely alternative.

Aside from the arbor, there is another garden feature you might want to consider adding for this occasion and beyond: a traditional garden bench or two. This will add a formal touch to your garden, as will a white Versailles pot of fuchsia or forsythia. To enhance the formality, have two of everything, with everything in balance. Espaliered fruit or a topiary, which would perhaps have to be ordered months in advance, will be a welcome source of formality and grace.

If you have a shady garden, it can overflow with variegated white-and-green ivy or hostas. Sprigs of dogwood or other flowering trees in vases—always balanced —will continue the theme of lush abundance. Blend the floral offerings on the tables with what is in the garden. If the bridesmaids are wearing teal blue and there are reds and whites in the garden, you will need to pull the two together. An arrangement of creamy roses with silvery, furry lamb's ears will do it. It is always lovely to duplicate the bridesmaids' bouquets at the tables, as well.

© Steven Mark Needham/Envision

BROILED JUMBO PRAWNS WITH HOT MUSTARD-MANGO SAUCE

50 jumbo prawns, peeled and deveined

10 large cloves garlic, crushed

1/4 cup olive oil

1 cup dry mustard

1 cup sugar

1 cup white wine vinegar

6 large egg yolks, lightly beaten

3 small ripe mangoes, peeled, pitted, and cut into chunks

Preheat broiler. In large mixing bowl, toss prawns with garlic and olive oil. Broil 3 to 5 minutes on each side, or until done. Reserve at room temperature.

In a double boiler, combine mustard, sugar, vinegar, and egg yolks over high heat. Stir constantly with a wire whisk until thickened, about 25 to 30 minutes. Be careful not to overcook or eggs will scramble. Remove from heat. Let cool to room temperature. In the bowl of a food processor, combine the mustard sauce with the mangoes and purée until smooth. Serve mustard-mango sauce in a dish near plate of prawns, so guests can dip prawns into sauce.

MINIATURE LAYERED VEGETABLE PASTRIES

3 cups all-purpose flour

2 teaspoons salt

1/2 cup grated Parmesan cheese

3/4 cup (1 1/2 sticks) cold butter

3 eggs, beaten

The Pea Layer

1/2 cup (1 stick) butter

2 tablespoons curry powder

1/4 cup minced onion

Two 10-ounce packages frozen peas, thawed and puréed

The Carrot Layer

3 tablespoons olive oil

1 large clove garlic, crushed

12 large carrots, trimmed, peeled, cooked, and puréed

3 tablespoons chopped fresh dill

2 teaspoons salt

1 teaspoon freshly ground black pepper

Dill sprigs, for garnish

Preheat oven to 400 degrees F. To make pastries, stir together flour, salt, and cheese in a bowl. Cut in ³/₄ cup butter until mixture resembles coarse oatmeal. Add eggs all at once. Stir with fork until dough holds together. Gather into small ball, cover completely with plastic wrap, and refrigerate 30 minutes.

Lightly grease 20 assorted miniature tart pans. Dust two sheets of wax paper with flour. Roll out pastry to ¹/₈-inch thickness between the two sheets. Peel off top sheet. Cut pastry into 20 rounds and fit into greased tart pans. Refrigerate 15 to 20 minutes. Prick pastry shells all over with fork. Bake on cookie sheet 10 to 15 minutes, until golden. Cool, then remove from pans.

To make vegetable fillings, melt ¹/₂ cup butter in a small skillet over medium-high heat. When hot, add curry powder and cook, stirring constantly, about 1 minute; add onion and continue to cook 1 to 2 minutes longer until onion is translucent. Stir in pea purée and cook an additional 3 minutes, until heated through. Reserve.

In another small skillet, heat oil over medium-high heat. When hot, cook garlic about 30 seconds. Stir in carrot purée and cook about 3 minutes longer. Stir in dill, salt, and pepper and cook an additional 3 to 5 minutes.

Spread a small amount of pea purée in bottom of each tart shell. Spread a small amount of carrot purée on top of peas. Garnish with small dill sprigs.

HONEY-AND-GRAIN MUSTARD MARINATED CORNISH GAME HENS

¹/₂ cup grainy mustard

¹/₂ cup cider vinegar

¹/₂ cup honey

¹/₄ cup chopped shallots

¹/₂ cup dry white wine

2 cups vegetable oil

¹/₄ cup chopped fresh thyme or 2 teaspoons dried

Salt and freshly ground pepper, to taste

25 Cornish game hens, split in half

Combine mustard, vinegar, honey, shallots, wine, oil, thyme, salt, and pepper in a large mixing bowl. Blend well.

Place hens in shallow pans, in one layer.* Cover with marinade. Refrigerate 6 to 8 hours or overnight, turning occasionally during that time.

Preheat oven to 375 degrees F. Bake 35 to 40 minutes, or until juices run clear when a small incision is made between the leg and the thigh. Most likely you will have to cook the hens in batches. To keep cooked chickens warm, cover completely with aluminum foil. Reheat, if necessary, 15 to 20 minutes before serving, or have a hot plate ready or chafing dish to keep cooked hens warm.

*If your refrigerator is too small to hold hens on sheet pans, use resealable plastic bags to marinate the hens in. This is a perfectly good alternative.

◄ An arching trellis covered with climbing roses is the perfect frame for a nuptial ceremony.

◄◄ This is an exquisite garden wedding cake by Cleaver and Company, one of New York's finest caterers.

SEARED TUNA SALAD

Fifteen 1-pound tuna steaks, about 2 inches thick
Freshly ground black pepper
Salt, to taste
4 cups extra virgin olive oil
30 cloves garlic, crushed

The Salad Dressing
10 whole shallots
1/2 cup firmly-packed tarragon leaves
1/2 cup Dijon-style mustard
1 1/2 cups tarragon vinegar
3 cups safflower or vegetable oil

The Salad
10 bunches watercress, trimmed
4 heads romaine
2 large heads radicchio
4 heads Boston lettuce
1 pound mâche
Lemon wedges, for garnish

Season the tuna steaks with enough black pepper to completely coat each side. Salt to taste. In a small bowl, combine olive oil and garlic. Pour over tuna and generously coat each side. Allow tuna to sit 5 minutes.

Meanwhile, heat 10-inch cast-iron skillet over high heat. Allow it to get very hot. Add tuna with olive oil and cook 2 to 3 minutes on each side (tuna should be rare inside). Remove tuna from heat, and allow it to stand 5 minutes before slicing. Slice into thin pieces and serve over mixed greens.

To make the dressing, combine shallots, tarragon, mustard, and vinegar in a very large mixing bowl. Whisk together. Continue whisking while slowly adding oil in a thin stream until well blended.

Combine salad ingredients. Serve sliced tuna on a platter with lemon wedges and salad in the middle.

The ingredients for an arbor wedding's table centerpieces might be a variation on the bouquets carried by the bridesmaids.

ARBOR PLANTS

If you plan ahead, your wedding could take place under a lushly covered arbor. This list is of particularly fast-growing climbing plants. These plants are also useful if you need to camouflage an eyesore near your garden. As the stems of twining plants grow, they twist and wrap themselves around the plant's support. Tendril plants produce slender, whiplike, woody appendages that curl around the garden support. Other plants must be tied to be trained to climb.

Bougainvillea glabra must be tied	zone 10	Bougainvillea
Clematis montana tendrils	zone 5	Clematis
Jasminum officinale twining	zone 7	Jasmine
Lonicera japonica 'Halliana' twining	zone 4	Hall's honeysuckle
Passiflora caerulea tendrils	zone 7–8	Passion-flower
Stephanotis floribunda tendrils	zone 10	Stephanotis
Bignonia capreolata tendrils	zone 6	Crossvine
Ipomoea purpurea twining	annual	Morning glory
Antigonon leptopus tendrils	zone 9	Coralvine
Wisteria floribunda twining	zone 4	Japanese wisteria
Clerodendrum tomsoniae twining	zone 9	Bleeding heart glory bower
Rosa wichuraiana must be tied	zone 5	Memorial rose

JUNE

Early-Season Salad Days
for Ten

* Cold Honeydew and Mango Soup
with Lime

*Sea Scallops with Oriental Pesto
Vinaigrette

Tomato-Basil Gelato

Bring out the earthenware, it is that kind of a celebration. Glass plates and bowls are called for, too, since one of the joys of early salad days is to see the crisp greens of earth's new gifts. Do not skimp on crocks of fresh herbed butter and an inventive assortment of breads, rolls, and crackers.

Vegetables are the featured players today. Create pretty patterns with the cut vegetables on a serving platter. Arrange bouquets of radishes to set amid the bowls of savory vegetable dips. Offer several kinds of freshly ground pepper and sea salt. And, yes, healthy new herbs of all kinds.

Early greens are a sort of triumph—they have come through. So what if they are not all *really* from your own garden. Be proud anyway, the feeling is contagious. Encourage people to create their own salads, to try all of early summer's offerings.

Today, the more edible the decoration, the better. Why not nibble on the nasturtiums? Leeks, radishes, green peppers, celery—what we call "crudites" at other times—are more than mere appetizers today; they are featured players. The variety of lettuces will fascinate and impress—mâche, mizunza, arugula, mustard, borage flowers, and whatever your garden and green market offer. Dessert fruits, too, take this fresh-from-the earth feeling a step further.

Have fun with table linens—perhaps a Portuguese or Dutch textile, or the right Hermes scarf. One thing your new garden does not need is competition, so think twice about using floral tablecloths and centerpieces today.

Homemade lemonade will be welcome, as will sparkling water and lime. And, instead of pouring from a wine bottle, perhaps you will choose a handsome pitcher or carafe, for that free, open feeling, the wine as light and crisp as the new harvest it is honoring and the warm bread it complements.

In the air today: soft fragrances and the sounds of sultry blues, light jazz, or Broadway's familiar, yet forever-friendly, favorites.

COLD HONEYDEW AND MANGO SOUP WITH LIME

1 large honeydew melon, peeled, seeded, cut into 2-inch (5-cm) chunks

2 large very ripe mangoes, peeled, seeded, cut into 1-inch (2.5-cm) cubes

Juice from 5 fresh limes, about ⅓ cup

Sliced limes, for garnish

Whipped cream, for garnish (optional)

In the bowl of a food processor, purée the honeydew. Transfer to a large bowl or soup tureen. Add the mangoes to the same processor and blend well until completely puréed. Combine mango

purée with melon purée. Add the lime juice. Blend well and chill for at least 4 hours. Garnish each bowl with a slice of lime and, for an added treat, a dollop of whipped cream.

© Brian Leatart

EDIBLE FLOWERS

There has been a recent awakening in awareness of the delicious possibilities from the garden. Here are some of our favorite edible flowers. Use them in salads to add color and surprising flavor. Or try them as a substitute for lettuce in sandwiches. Experiment with them in many ways until you find the best complements for their sometimes unusual flavors. However, always remember that some flowers and plants are poisonous when consumed (see our list that follows), and check carefully before you move beyond the list below.

Pimpinella anisum	annual	Anise Hyssop
Laurus nobilis	zone 7	Bay Laurel
Monarda didyma	zone 4	Bee balm
Borago officinalis	annual	Borage
Chamaemelum nobile	zone 4	Chamomile
Allium schoenoprasum	zone 2–3	Chive
Hemerocallis hybrids		Daylily
Taraxacum officinale	zone 3	Dandelion
Pelargonium hybrids		Scented geranium
Alcea rosea	zone 2–3	Hollyhock
Lavandula angustifolia	zone 5	English lavender
Tagetes patula	annual	Marigold
Brassica juncea	annual	Mustard
Tropaeolum majus	annual	Nasturium
Origanum vulgare	zone 3	Marjorum
Viola x wittrockiana	annual	Pansy
Rosa species		Rose
Rosmarinus officinalis	zone 6	Rosemary
Satureja montana	zone 5	Winter savory

© Brian Leatart

© Anita Sabarese

SEA SCALLOPS WITH ORIENTAL PESTO VINAIGRETTE

2 scallions, thinly sliced

¹/₄ cup chopped fresh cilantro

2 tablespoons minced peeled fresh gingerroot

2 cloves garlic, crushed

Juice from 1 lime

¹/₄ cup rice wine vinegar

3 tablespoons low-sodium soy sauce

1 tablespoon sugar

1 teaspoon salt

³/₄ cup vegetable oil

¹/₂ teaspoon crushed Sichaun peppercorns

Assorted greens, such as mâche, mizunza, arugula, endive, mustard, borage flowers, baby lettuces and a variety of fresh herbs

4 pounds sea scallops

Salt and pepper, to taste

In a small bowl, combine scallions, cilantro, ginger, garlic, lime juice, vinegar, soy sauce, sugar, and salt. Beat together with a wire whisk. Slowly, in a thin stream, beat in ¹/₂ cup oil until it is well blended. Add the peppercorns. Toss dressing with the salad greens and reserve.

In a 12-inch skillet, heat the remaining ¹/₄ cup oil over high heat. When hot, add the scallops. Season with salt and pepper to taste. Cook 7 to 10 minutes depending on size of scallops. Serve over pesto-coated greens.

TOXIC, POISONOUS FLOWERS

Be careful when you experiment with edible plants and flowers—SOME ARE POISONOUS. Here is a list of the most common garden plants that are harmful. However, check every type of plant before you serve it to your guests or eat it yourself.

Dicentra species	Bleeding Heart
Delphinium species	Delphinium
Digitalis purpurea	Foxglove
Hydrangea species	Hydrangea
Aconitum napellus	Monkshood
Narcissus species	Daffodil
Nerium oleander	Oleander
Vinca species	Periwinkle
Euphorbia pulcherrima	Poinsettia
Primula species	Primrose

◄ ▲ **Nasturtium blossoms add summery color and a peppery flavor, not unlike watercress, to garden party dishes.**

◄ **Using flowers as food is very much in vogue— but only from pesticide-free gardens, please. Bright blue, cucumber-flavored borage in lemonade and other drinks; early chive blossoms floated in soup, hidden in omelets, scattered on salads; sweet violets, pansies, day lily petals, and squash blossoms are all a delight to the eye as well as the tastebuds. Don't use roadside or florists' flowers, though.**

JUNE

Classic Dinner
for Four

*Cold Purée of Watercress Soup
*Cinnamon-Spiced Chicken
*Orange Rice with Lemon Thyme
*Roasted Pepper Melange
Raspberry Mousse with Crème Chantilly

Here is a gracious dinner party perfect for entertaining with reserve and elegance. For this event, you will not be getting up and down to serve, however well you do it. You want to put the pieces in place and let the evening roll forward. Competent help is what you will need: help with the children, perhaps help with your lawn and garden, as well as with the preparation and presentation of the food and drink. With quiet contemporary or light classical music playing, and your garden as impeccable as it has ever been, you will be needed at the table to enjoy and enhance the conversation, to effortlessly walk that subtle line joining business

with pleasure, offering both.

The setting will be sleek and serene, a good time to prove that business does not have to be boring, calculated, or austere. The point of the evening is to get your point across, whether to a boss or a client. You want your garden to take on the aura of an impressive, expensive restaurant for this evening but more personal and distinctive.

Lacy cloths and fancily folded napkins are as outré for this meal as glitz, glamour, and big centerpieces. Instead, you will be more comfortable with a tablecloth or place mats of linen, and perhaps pastels instead of formal white. Scandinavian-style oil lamps at different heights, offering a steady, protected light instead of candles, would have a pleasing, no-nonsense charm.

This is definitely the evening for an expensive bottle of wine—but not an ostentatious one. Do not leave the choice up to your liquor store, but do your own research, and perhaps even find out a few wonderful things about the wine's year. As for hard liquors, the very best is best tonight, since that is what is served on business occasions at high levels.

Lulls in conversation are deadly on such an evening, and there will be other subjects broached besides business, so think of good talk as your main entree, and all else will follow.

Since the conversation may peak with the mellow after-coffee hour, pay as much attention to that course as to any other. Cappuccino and espresso, with attendant liqueurs, are expected and appreciated, as they are in fine restaurants.

COLD PURÉE OF WATERCRESS SOUP

1 tablespoon extra virgin olive oil

½ medium onion, finely chopped

1 large clove garlic, crushed

2 bunches fresh watercress (about 2 cups), washed and trimmed

¼ cup chopped fresh chervil

½ teaspoon fresh thyme leaves or ¼ teaspoon dried

½ teaspoon freshly ground black pepper

½ teaspoon salt

2 cups chicken broth

2 tablespoons crème fraîche

In a 3-quart saucepan, heat oil over high heat. Add onion. Cook, stirring constantly, 3 to 5 minutes.

Add garlic. Cook, stirring constantly, an additional 30 seconds.

Add watercress and chervil. Cook 2 to 3 minutes, until the greens begin to wilt.

Add thyme, pepper, salt, and chicken broth. Bring to boil. Reduce heat to low and simmer 20 to 25 minutes. Remove from heat.

Purée in food processor or blender until smooth. Chill thoroughly. Before serving, add crème fraîche and blend well.

Fine conversation will be on the menu tonight, as will a superbly appropriate wine and careful attention to every delicious detail of this intimate dinner.

CINNAMON-SPICED CHICKEN

1 cup dry sherry
1 tablespoon ground cinnamon
¹/2 cup honey
¹/4 cup fresh-squeezed lime juice
1 large clove garlic, minced
1 teaspoon salt
1¹/2 teaspoons freshly ground black pepper
*Two 2- to 2¹/2-pound chickens, cut into
    quarters*

In a large mixing bowl, combine sherry,
cinnamon, honey, lime juice, garlic, salt,
and pepper.

Arrange chicken pieces in a single
layer in a shallow ovenproof pan. Pour
marinade over chicken. Turn pieces to
coat well. Cover with plastic wrap.
Refrigerate overnight or longer, if
desired.

Preheat oven to 350 degrees F.
Drain marinade and reserve. Bake
chicken for 40 to 50 minutes, depending on size of pieces. Baste with marinade and turn chicken pieces once or
twice during the cooking process.

NOTE: This dish is also wonderful
grilled over charcoal. Grill over
medium-high heat, 15 to 20 minutes for
breast pieces, 20 to 25 minutes for
thigh or leg portions.

© Derek Fell

ORANGE RICE WITH LEMON THYME

1 tablespoon unsalted butter
¹/₂ cup finely chopped onion
2 large cloves garlic, crushed
1 tablespoon finely chopped fresh lemon thyme or regular thyme or ¹/₄ teaspoon dried
1 teaspoon poultry seasoning
1 teaspoon salt
1 cup white rice
One 13³/₄-ounce can low-sodium chicken broth
Juice and grated rind from 3 small oranges

In a 1-quart saucepan fitted with lid, melt butter over high heat. Add onion and cook, stirring constantly, 1 to 2 minutes. Add garlic, thyme, poultry seasoning, and salt. Cook 1 to 2 minutes longer. Add rice. Stir to coat thoroughly.

Stir in broth, orange juice, and rind. Bring to boil. Cover and reduce heat to low, and simmer 20 to 25 minutes, or until all liquid has been absorbed and rice is tender. Turn off heat. Keep covered for an additional 5 minutes. Stir and serve.

◄ Garden partygivers are forever on the lookout for interesting statuary and containers, offering an element of surprise to their guests and points of focus to their gardens.

► Vegetables have a definite beauty of their own, and served simply in the luscious green setting of your garden, they are particularly delectable.

ABOUT WATERCRESS

Nasturium officinale aquatic   zone 4   Watercress

Watercress is a member of the mustard family, and it grows well in shallow water, preferably cold and flowing. It can also be grown in containers, as long as it is watered often and thoroughly, into a pot liner as well as from the top of the pot. It is easily rooted from stems. The leaves are especially good as a salad in the early spring.

ROASTED PEPPER MELANGE

3 large red bell peppers
3 large yellow peppers
3 large green bell peppers
Olive oil, to coat, plus 1 tablespoon
3 tablespoons red wine vinegar
¹/₄ cup chopped fresh basil leaves
1 large clove garlic, minced
¹/₄ teaspoon salt
¹/₂ teaspoon cracked black pepper
Grated Parmesan cheese (optional)

Preheat broiler. Wash peppers and dry thoroughly. Rub each pepper with enough olive oil to coat. Char peppers under broiler, turning several times until all sides are completely blackened. Place charred peppers in a large paper bag and seal. Allow them to sit and steam for 10 to 15 minutes. When peppers are cool enough to handle, peel them, discard core and seeds, and cut into thin strips.

Place peppers in large serving bowl. Combine with 1 tablespoon olive oil, vinegar, basil, garlic, salt, and pepper. Serve warm. Sprinkle with a little freshly grated Parmesan cheese, if desired.

© Michael Skott

JULY

Elegant Thirties Soiree
for Six

Tea-Smoked Salmon with Ginger Butter

Quail Stuffed with Wild Rice and Nasturtiums

String Beans Vinaigrette

Poires Helene

Rum Punch

For this party, atmosphere counts for everything. Either research and prepare a flawless tape of the decade's music or, by all means, consider hiring a compact disc jockey, and supply a platform for romantic dancing to Cole Porter music.

The attitude for this evening: light and even slightly campy. Research and read about this incredible era so you can supply stories to enthrall your guests. Toss off one juicy scandal after another. We are between the wars tonight, and laughter is everything. We are mobsters, molls, and elite society, too. This party is a movable feast, the silver moon, and a Gershwin tune.

Tonight create dramatic Ikebana arrangements using irises and grasses. Or create an exotic centerpiece of orchids, birds of paradise, or lilies.

Spread the tables with the tall, bold gladiolas so popular in the thirties. Sheer white linen tablecloths are in order, combined with blue, gray, or pink napkins that are scalloped or perhaps embroidered around the edges.

For china, search out plates with silver or gold rims. Silver or crystal candlesticks will do you proud in the company of the evening's beaded, sleeveless cocktail dresses or the basic black pioneered by Coco Chanel during this adventurous age.

For tonight, three tables of ten each and unimpeded views of all the guests will ensure the scintillating conversation you are provoking at every turn.

Exotic foods beckon from silver trays. Tonight there *is* a reason for servers to wear white gloves when they present the fluted glasses of champagne or the Rum Punch, Manhattans, and Singapore Slings that prepared us for the foreboding forties.

Not only the clothes, but the attitude of the thirties should be onstage tonight, reminding all of when dancers touched, stockings gleamed, partygoers laughed merrily, and unforgettable music accompanied all.

TEA-SMOKED SALMON WITH GINGER BUTTER

1/2 cup kosher salt
1/2 cup granulated sugar
1 cup Lapsang Souchong tea leaves
1 pound salmon fillet, with skin attached

The Butter
1/4 cup (1/2 stick) unsalted butter, softened
1 1-inch piece fresh gingerroot, peeled and grated
Black bread
Lemon wedges (optional)

In a small bowl, combine salt, sugar, and tea leaves. Mix thoroughly. Place about 1/2 cup of the salt/tea mixture on the bottom of a large plate. Place the salmon fillet, skin side down, on the salt. Spread the rest of the mixture on top of the salmon's flesh side. Cover with plastic wrap and weight it down with a heavy pot or several dishes. Refrigerate for 48 hours, turning the salmon once or twice during this time. To serve, rinse the salmon of all salt and tea leaves. Slice into paper thin slices. Serve on black bread spread with ginger butter.

To make the butter, combine softened butter with ginger. Blend well and spread thinly on black bread with crusts removed. Cut into triangles. Top with the salmon and serve with lemon wedges.

QUAIL STUFFED WITH WILD RICE AND NASTURTIUMS

4 tablespoons (1/2 stick) unsalted butter
1 cup minced onion
4 large cloves garlic, crushed
1/2 teaspoon freshly ground black pepper
6 ounces wild rice
3 cups chicken broth
1/2 pound chicken livers
2 cups chopped arugula leaves
3 cups nasturtium flowers
Salt, to taste
12 whole quails
Salt and pepper
Melted butter

Preheat oven to 375 degrees F. In a 1-quart saucepan fitted with lid, melt 2 tablespoons butter over high heat. When hot, add onion. Cook, stirring constantly, until onion becomes translucent. Add garlic and cook an additional 30 seconds. Add black pepper and rice. Stir to coat. Add broth. Bring to boil. Cover. Reduce heat to low and simmer 45 minutes or until rice is tender but not mushy. If necessary, strain rice of excess liquid in colander. Transfer rice to large mixing bowl and cool completely.

Meanwhile, in a small skillet, melt remaining 2 tablespoons butter over high heat. When hot, cook chicken livers 5 to 7 minutes. Allow them to cool enough so that they are easy to handle. Cut into small pieces and add to rice along with any of the cooking liquid. Stir in arugula and nasturtiums. Season with salt to taste.

Season quail inside and out with salt and pepper. Divide stuffing equally among all the quail. Truss if desired. Arrange quail in a deep roasting pan. Brush with a little melted butter. Bake 25 to 30 minutes, basting occasionally with any of the pan juices.

RUM PUNCH

5 ounces dark Jamaican rum

5 ounces vodka

2¹/₂ cups light rum

1 ounce frozen concentrate for daiquiri mix

1 ounce frozen concentrate for orange juice

1 ounce frozen concentrate for lemonade

¹/₂ fresh pineapple, cut into small chunks

1 cup fresh strawberries, cut in half

Mint leaves, for garnish

Combine all ingredients in a large punch bowl. Blend well with an electric mixer or whisk. Serve in tall glasses and garnish with mint leaves.

▲▶ An ikebana arrangement can be as simple, but evocative, as one blossom floating in a glass bowl. Put one at each place setting as a special gift to your guests.

© Bo Parker

IKEBANA

Ikebana is the Oriental tradition of highly structured floral arrangement infused with symbolism. Generally, the components of the arrangement are positioned to reflect the natural world—Heaven, Man, and Earth. The design of an Ikebana arrangement seems very simple, though it is actually very carefully put together. However, any arranger can be inspired by the beautiful designs and the principles.

Ikebana arrangements often feature one dramatic flower. Here is a list of our favorites, any of which will add a touch of the exotic in keeping with your Thirties theme. Many of these plants are tropical, so they will be difficult for you to grow. However, your florist can get them for you, though you may need to order them in advance.

Spathiphyllum floribundum	zone 10	Spathiphyllum
Zantedeschia aethiopica	zone 10	Calla lily
Strelitzia reginae	zone 10	Queen's bird-of-paradise
Canna x generalis	zone 9	Canna
Papaver orientale	zone 2–3	Oriental poppy
Clivia miniata	zone 10	Scarlet kafir-lily
Oncidium papilio	zone 10	Butterfly orchid
Cymbidium insigne	zone 10	Cymbidium orchid
Phalaenopsis 'Doris'	zone 10	Doris orchid
Cattleya labiata	zone 10	Cattleya lily
Gardenia jasminoides	zone 8–9	Gardenia
Agapanthus orientalis	zone 9	Oriental agapanthus

JULY

Midsummer Night's Late Supper

for Eight

Wild Mushroom Vichyssoise
Fillet of Salmon Poached with Fresh Lovage
Tian de Courgettes
Assorted Melon Salad with Fresh Coriander

Before you invite anyone to your Midsummer Night's Late Supper, commission a tarot reader, a ballgazer, a palmist, a diviner of any sort, or perhaps a magician. Collect several different renditions of "Au Clair de Lune" to play at different times during the evening, and reread Shakespeare's great play.

Why not ask your guests to come as their own mistaken identities, the people they have always wanted to be? Tempt them by promising they will assume that identity at midnight.

Fill the punch bowl with a magical concoction that will assist this transformation, but do not reveal the ingredients.

For tonight, perhaps a long table that accommodates everybody would be perfect, for you do not want the magical energy scattered. Shakespearean flowers in little groupings at each—or every second or third—place setting will enhance the mood. In his plays, poems, and sonnets, the Bard names 180 different plants, the most famous collection in *A Midsummer Night's Dream* (see box).

Incorporate as many of these flowers as you can into your garden and table decor. Add to this atmosphere the flickering of scented candles. This is the night to place a shimmery, flowing fabric over the dining table—not a tent, but a mere gossamer creation that will embrace the soft light of floating candles and admit the glow of the torches placed outside. After all, this is a fairy play written for the celebrations connected to a real wedding, at a time when gardens still retained protective walls and arbors were planted with trees and climbers entwining overhead, offering a sense of intimacy you might want to duplicate.

Delicate floral china is in order. Lush, glossy leaves are called for tonight, as well as flowers. The table must be generously strewn with them. If pansies, artfully placed, will survive, they are perfect, since they are the magical "little western flower" used by Oberon to cast a spell on Titania the Fairy Queen.

Elizabethan dancing music and spirited, slightly dangerous, gypsy tunes will give the cocktail hour the compelling energy that will send the evening twirling into dinner. You are, after all, celebrating theater.

By all means, translate your gracious invitations into Shakespearean verse, so that the expectant guests entering your garden are prepared to become players, as well as charmed guests. If you cannot write the verse yourself, think about enlisting the services of an English or theater teacher; there is always a bard lurking before the blackboard.

The varying flavors of different types of mushrooms are fascinating to explore. Be very, very careful if you are collecting from the wild.

A SHAKESPEARE GARDEN

I know a bank where the wild thyme blows,
Where oxlips and the nodding violet grows,
Quite over-canopied with luscious woodbine,
With sweet musk-roses with eglantine.
There sleeps Titania sometime of the night,
Lull'd in these flowers with dances and delight.

William Shakespeare
A Midsummer Night's Dream

Feature flowers from the play in the arrangements that decorate your tables and party setting.

Wild thyme:	*Thymus nitidus*	zone 5	Sicily thyme
Oxlip:	*Primula vulgaris*	zone 5	English primrose
Nodding violet:	*Viola odorata*	zone 6	Sweet violet
Woodbine:	*Lonicera periclymenum*	zone 4	Honeysuckle
Musk-rose:	*Rosa moschata nastarana*	zone 6	Persian musk rose
Eglantine:	*Rosa eglanteria*	zone 4	Sweet brier rose

Each of these flowers has adopted a special meaning over time. Share their messages with your guests.

Primrose: innocence
Violet: humility
Honeysuckle: fidelity
Rose: love and rebirth

© Dennis Gottlieb

WILD MUSHROOM VICHYSSOISE

2 tablespoons unsalted butter

5 large shallots, minced

2 leeks, washed and thinly sliced, white part only

4 large cloves garlic, minced

$^1/_2$ pound shiitake mushrooms, stemmed, plus 8 cut into julienne sticks for garnish

$^1/_2$ pound oyster mushrooms, stemmed

8 large new potatoes, peeled and cut in half

Four 13$^3/_4$-ounce cans low-sodium chicken broth

1 cup milk

Salt and freshly ground black pepper, to taste

$^1/_4$ cup chopped fresh chives

In a 3-quart saucepan fitted with lid, melt butter over high heat. Add shallots and leeks and cook, stirring constantly, until leeks are softened, about 3 to 5 minutes. Add garlic and continue stirring about 30 seconds longer. Stir 1 minute longer. Add mushrooms and potatoes. Reduce heat to medium and cook about 3 minutes.

Add broth. Bring to boil over high heat. Reduce heat to low, cover and cook 20 to 25 minutes, until potatoes are tender. Purée entire contents in the bowl of a food processor or blender until smooth. Add milk, and season with salt and pepper. Refrigerate 6 to 8 hours, until thoroughly chilled and flavors have had a chance to develop. Garnish with chives before serving.

The Folger Shakespeare Library

FILLET OF SALMON POACHED WITH FRESH LOVAGE

4 cups fish stock or broth

1 teaspoon whole black peppercorns

$^1/_2$ teaspoon salt

4 large sprigs fresh lovage

Eight 6-ounce salmon fillets

2 tablespoons unsalted butter, at room temperature

Chopped fresh parsley (optional)

In a 12-inch skillet over high heat, combine the stock, peppercorns, salt, and lovage. Bring to boil. Reduce heat to medium and simmer 5 to 10 minutes.

Add the fillets in a single layer to the pan and cover (it will probably be necessary to cook the fish in two batches). Cook 5 to 7 minutes, until flesh flakes easily with a fork. Remove fish with a slotted spatula to drain off poaching liquid. Transfer to serving platter. Cover with aluminum foil to keep warm while cooking remaining fillets. When all fish has been cooked, increase heat to medium-high and continue cooking poaching liquid, uncovered, until reduced by one-third. Strain broth through a fine-meshed sieve. Whisk in butter. Taste and correct seasonings. Pour over salmon and garnish with chopped parsley, if desired.

ABOUT LOVAGE

Levisticum officinale   zone 6   Lovage

Lovage is a member of the carrot family, but its leaves most resemble those of celery. Its aromatic seeds have been used for centuries in sweets and cordials, but it has recently been recognized as a good substitute for salt. It makes a fragrant tea and can replace celery in many recipes. It is a handsome plant, especially as a background in a floral border, so you will enjoy growing your own lovage.

TIAN DE COURGETTES

3 medium red bell peppers

6 medium yellow summer squash

6 medium zucchini

4 to 5 large red ripe tomatoes

1 large onion, thinly sliced

¹/₃ plus ¹/₄ cup extra virgin olive oil

¹/₂ cup water

8 large cloves garlic, crushed

Salt and pepper, to taste

1 tablespoon chopped fresh thyme or
*   ¹/₄ teaspoon dried*

Preheat broiler. Roast peppers, turning several times, until black on all sides. Peel and discard seeds and core. Slice peppers into thin strips. Trim off the ends of the yellow squash and cut into ¹/₄-inch-thick slices. Repeat this procedure with the zucchini. Remove cores from tomatoes and cut into ¹/₄-inch thick slices.

In a 10-inch skillet over high heat, combine onion with ¹/₃ cup olive oil and the water. Cook until tender, about 3 to 5 minutes. Drain.

Heat oven to 350 degrees F. Put onions on the bottom of a 9-inch × 13-inch ovenproof casserole. Put garlic and pepper strips on top of the onions. Then make a layer of tomatoes, followed by a layer of zucchini, followed by a layer of yellow squash. Sprinkle with salt and pepper to taste and thyme.

Drizzle remaining ¹/₄ cup olive oil over top. Bake for 30 minutes, then press vegetables down with the back of a spatula. Raise temperature of oven to 475 degrees F and bake for 15 minutes, or until mixture is black on top.

AUG

*Rosemary Scones

Assorted Tea Sandwiches

*Cold Breast of Duck with Oriental Citrus
Glaze

Cheese and Fruit Platter

Individual Fruit and Custard Tarts

It helps to have a Victorian house, but faux Victoriana may be even more fun. Start by overdoing everything.

If you are thinking "formal," remember that it was the Victorians who converted the hammock to garden use, discovered the sprightly, nonsensical operettas of Gilbert and Sullivan, and delighted in euphonious barbershop quartets. The focus of any Victorian event was "the pleasure of company," pure and simple. That was the only simple thing about the age, however. Creative, cozy clutter was the keynote of style. Victorians were obsessed with details, and every one you include today, from palm fronds to stuffed birds, will add to this tea party's charm. Create a Victorian still-life centerpiece, overflowing with flowers, grapes, cherries, and anything else you have on hand. You can also pile fruit high in a pedestal bowl, or spread it from a cornucopia.

Though meat in the sandwiches distinguishes "High Tea" from the other kind, it is really the tarts that will make your day worthy of the name. Custard and fruit, scones and butter will set the tone, as will the cut glass carafes and delicate china settings you bring out for your Tea. Polish up the ornate silver, and press and present the fine and lacy antique cloths that are fit for a queen. And for seating, wicker and bentwood furniture set the proper mood.

Out on the lawn, a game of croquet will continue the Victorian tone, to the tune of mallets softly tapping colorful balls through wire wickets. Croquet is at once civilized and competitive, always a wonderful way to socialize.

© Michael Grand

© Steven Mark Needham/Envision

ROSEMARY SCONES

1³/4 cups all-purpose flour

2¹/4 teaspoons double-acting baking powder

2 tablespoons sugar

¹/2 teaspoon salt

¹/4 cup (¹/2 stick) cold butter

2 eggs

¹/3 cup light cream

*2 tablespoons finely chopped fresh rosemary
    or ¹/2 teaspoon dried*

Sugar for garnish

Preheat oven to 450 degrees F. In a large mixing bowl, sift together the flour, baking powder, sugar, and salt. Using a pastry blender, cut in the butter until the size of small peas.

In a separate bowl, beat the eggs. Remove 2 tablespoons of the eggs to brush scones before baking. Add cream to the remainder. Make a well in the center of the dry ingredients. Pour liquid into it. Add rosemary. Combine with a few swift strokes. Do not overmix.

Turn the dough out onto a lightly floured board. Pat down to 3/4-inch thickness. Cut with a knife into diamond shapes or rounds. Brush with reserved egg and sprinkle with sugar. Bake about 15 minutes.

COLD BREAST OF DUCK WITH ORIENTAL CITRUS GLAZE

Juice from 3 lemons

Juice from 3 limes

1 cup orange juice

1 cup honey

1 teaspoon hot bean paste

¹/3 cup balsamic vinegar

¹/4 cup low-sodium soy sauce

2 tablespoons chopped fresh gingerroot

4 large cloves garlic, crushed

One 13³/4-ounce can chicken broth

¹/4 teaspoon Oriental five-spice seasoning

8 whole boneless duck breasts

3 oranges, sliced for garnish

2 bunches scallions, for garnish

In a large 8-quart saucepot fitted with lid, combine the lemon, lime and orange juices, honey, bean paste, vinegar, soy sauce, ginger, garlic, broth, and five-spice seasoning. Reserve.

In a 12-inch skillet over high heat, place duck when pan is very hot, skin side down. Brown very well on both sides, about 5 to 7 minutes on each side. Transfer cooked duck to saucepot with marinade. When all the duck has been browned and added to marinade, bring to boil over high heat. Cover. Reduce heat to low and simmer 30 minutes. Transfer duck to platter. Reserve. Increase heat and reduce marinade by two-thirds or until it becomes syrupy, about 25 to 30 minutes. Pour sauce over duck and toss to coat thoroughly. Chill well before serving. Garnish with orange slices and scallions.

© Edmund Nagele/FPG International

LAWNS AND SHADE TREES

Your guests will want to stroll across your lawn, parasols in hand, after they have had their Victorian tea under a shady tree. Here are some suggestions, organized regionally, for the best lawn grasses.

Zones 8 to 10, dry regions
    Bermuda
    Centipede
Zone 10, humid regions
    St. Augustine
    Bahia
Zone 4 to 7
    Cool weather grasses
    Bluegrass
    Kentucky
Zone 7 to 9
    Warm season grasses
    Bermuda
    Zoysia

These are a few classic shade trees.

Fagus sylvatica 'Pendula'	zone 4	Weeping English Beech
Salix alba 'Tristis'	zone 2	Golden weeping willow
Quercus rubra	zone 3	Red Oak
Gleditsia triancanthos	zone 4	Honey locust
Prosopsis glandulosa glandulosa	zone 8	Honey mesquite
Betula lenta	zone 3	Sweet birch
Ginkgo biloba	zone 4	Ginkgo
Liriodendron tulipfera	zone 4	Tulip tree

AUG

Meteor Shower Party
for Six

Blue Moon Mixers
Crunchy Squid
Baked Tomato Craters
Star Fruit Salad with Ginger-Rum Glaze

Was there ever a better moment for the fragrant "Stargazer" lily? Tonight you are navigating by the stars, steering this celebration to the heavens and back home. You will welcome all the help you can gather: sparklers for the desserts, Mylar stars and glowing moons hung to dance in the trees, "place maps" showing constellations and star charts, lighted cosmic globes.

Borrow a high-powered telescope from an astronomy teacher or an astronomer. You will need someone to point out the meteors, so why not try to borrow the expert along with the telescope? A contribution to his or her school or special project might be all the enticement such a galactic techie needs.

Seek out and buy holographic objects and send them home with guests as favors. Raid the children's space toys.

Shamelessly borrow from their musical collections, too. *Star Trek* and *Star Wars* themes are a must. Handel's "Planets" and the theme from *2001* will also evoke the right mood. There are endless—and endlessly varied—musical possibilities. Dancing will be impromptu, and is guaranteed to begin with the first bars of "Moon River" and "Stardust."

Find out the astrological signs of the guests and find sticker versions of their symbols; attach them to each guest as he or she arrives and watch the Sagittarians hailing each other merrily across the room as they lift off with their Blue Moon Mixers.

You can have a great deal of fun planning this star-watching party; nothing is too farfetched, or outlandish. Your guests, after all, will be expecting a cosmic, heavenly time. They should come dressed informally, and each should bring a sweater. They might very well, after all, wind up lying flat out on the lawn, gazing upward. A few cafe tables with two to four wrought-iron or other informal chairs should be all you need to accommodate them happily.

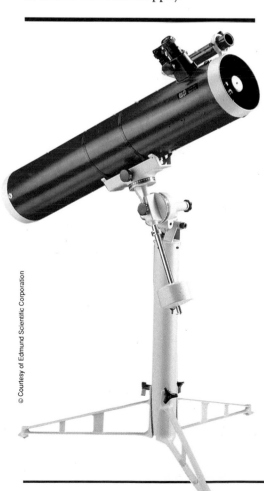

© Courtesy of Edmund Scientific Corporation

BLUE MOON MIXERS

9 ounces dry vermouth
9 ounces curaçao
9 ounces light rum
1 teaspoon grenadine
3 ounces lemon juice
Orange peel for garnish

Combine all ingredients in a large pitcher and chill thoroughly. Serve in chilled glasses with a twist of orange peel.

CRUNCHY SQUID

1 pound squid, combination of bodies and
*   tentacles*
³/4 cup all-purpose flour
1 teaspoon salt
¹/2 teaspoon black pepper
2 large eggs
1¹/2 cups seasoned dry bread crumbs
1 tablespoon dried oregano
2 teaspoons dried thyme
Vegetable oil
Lemon wedges
Chopped parsley for garnish (optional)

Slice squid bodies crosswise into rings. Cut the tentacles if they are too long. Combine flour, salt, and pepper in a shallow dish. In another shallow dish, beat eggs to blend well. Combine bread crumbs with oregano and thyme in still another dish. Roll squid in flour mixture a few pieces at a time, dip in beaten

eggs allowing excess to drip back into dish, then roll in crumb mixture and coat well.

Arrange crumb-coated squid on a baking sheet or flat platter. At this point you can cover and refrigerate until ready to cook.

In a deep, heavy-gauged saucepot, heat about two inches oil to 375 degrees F on a deep-fat fry thermometer or until a 1-inch cube of bread browns in 1 minute. Add squid, a few pieces at a time, and cook until just golden brown on all sides. *Don't overcook or squid will toughen.*

Remove from oil with slotted spoon. Drain well on paper towels. Serve with lemon wedges. Sprinkle with chopped parsley, if desired.

BAKED TOMATO CRATERS

12 to 15 cloves garlic, sliced
5 medium-size ripe tomatoes
1 cup parsley leaves
¹/2 cup seasoned dry bread crumbs
¹/4 cup grated Parmesan cheese
¹/2 teaspoon salt
¹/2 teaspoon freshly ground black pepper
¹/4 cup extra virgin olive oil

Preheat oven to 350 degrees F. In a 1-quart saucepot over high heat, place 2 cups water. Bring to boil. Add garlic slices and blanch 1 minute. Drain in colander, and rinse in colander under cold water. Cut tomatoes in half horizontally. Arrange tomatoes, cut side up, in a shallow baking pan. Stick garlic slices into tomatoes so that they stick up out of each tomato half.

In the bowl of a food processor, combine parsley, bread crumbs, cheese, salt, pepper, and olive oil. Process until parsley leaves are finely minced. Divide the cheese-crumb mixture evenly among all the tomatoes. Bake 10 to 15 minutes, or until tomatoes are slightly soft to the touch (doneness will depend greatly on how ripe the tomatoes are). Finish under the broiler 1 to 2 minutes, or until bread crumb mixture becomes golden brown.

STAR FRUIT SALAD WITH GINGER-RUM GLAZE

¹/₄ cup sugar

¹/₂ cup water

¹/₄ cup dark rum

2 tablespoons finely minced candied ginger

10 ripe star fruit, peeled and cut into ¹/₄-inch-thick slices

In a medium-size saucepan over high heat, combine sugar, water, rum, and ginger. Bring to boil. Reduce heat to medium. Simmer and cook 10 to 15 minutes, or until it takes on a syrupy consistency. Allow syrup to cool 10 minutes. Pour over star fruit. Toss to coat. Chill at least 1 hour or overnight. Note: This is a real treat served over ice cream.

PLANTS OF THE FUTURE

The theme of a meteor shower party invites unusual or futuristic plants. Plant them in containers and set them in the middle of the tables or around the edges of your party area. Here are some suggestions, or choose your favorites.

Allium giganteum　　zone 5　　Giant onion
Three- to five-foot slender stalk ends in a bright blue-purple ball. Blooming in summer, these stunning flowers are excellent for drying; feature in arrangements all year 'round.

Eucomis comosa　　zone 7　　Pineapple Flower
A member of the lily flower, this plant resembles the fruit. If you live north of zone 7, it may be cultivated indoors.

Darwin tulip 'La Tulipe Noire'
A dark, deep purple, almost black. Force them in containers and set one in the center of each table.

There are many unusual plants among the cactus and succulents. These are just a few:

Stapelia hirsuta　　zone 10　　Shaggy stapelia
A desert plant with dark purple-brown flowers with line of cream or purple and pale purplish leaves.

Lithops lesliei　　zone 10　　Living stones
This succulent is so named because the plant resembles, in size and shape, small stones, with yellow or white flowers emerging from the line in the middle of the plant. After these succulents flower from summer to fall, do not give them *any* water until the following spring (about six months).

Aeonium arboreum　　zone 9　　Black Rose
Succulent leaves form a deep magenta rosette. This plant needs hot, summer sun.

For added eerie attraction, feature insect-eating plants in terrariums. You may or may not want to dare your guests to feed them.

Dionaea muscipula　　zone 8　　Venus flytrap
Movement on this plant's sensitive leaves causes the leaf to close and trap the hapless insect inside.

AUG

Dewy Saturday Morning Breakfast
for Six

Soft Boiled Eggs
*Raspberry Muffins with Sweet Mint Butter
*Veal Sausage En Croûte with Peach Syrup
Frozen Orange and Strawberry Frappes

For this repast, bring out fresh table linens and make a sprightly bouquet of summer flowers. Your table should say, "Good morning," but not too loudly. It is, after all, Saturday and the ambience is one of ease and casual comfort.

One of the secrets of a big, abundant, friendly breakfast served by an unhassled host or hostess is that many of the menu items can be cooked ahead and kept warm. Not indefinitely, of course, but a well-organized, confident cook can present goodies made at dawn as if they just came out of the oven.

The most marvelous way to welcome a breakfast guest is with the smell of fresh coffee, so go all out there. Add vanilla or cinnamon or, better yet, offer a fragrant variety. Invite your guests to try them all. Do not forget to emphasize wonderful teas, including herbal types, and decaffeinated coffee, as well.

Some people take longer than others to wake up, and some are lost without a morning paper, so why not supply at least one? If you live in a big city, how thoughtful and conversation-provoking to send someone out for different morning papers from faraway places, the more exotic the better. Compare the news of the day.

If there is to be music, be careful. Go lightly rather than

sprightly: accessible jazz and Mozart are nice choices.

Because this is a garden breakfast, fresh herbs will be great performers: in eggs, on potatoes, or in mint butter. Keep a hot pot filled with water at a side table so guests can boil their own eggs. "Fresh" applies as well to butter and peach syrup, those indispensable breakfast ingredients. Lucky you are if the peaches, strawberries, and raspberries in this menu come from your own garden. And jams! Remember the unusual but inviting jar from Aunt Constance you received last Christmas? Now is the time to break it open.

Fresh-squeezed juice is also unbeatable. Just as you would assign a friend to be bartender at an evening party, have someone on hand to do the honors. Give a new taste to orange juice when you blend it with strawberries.

© Tyler Gearhart/Envision

▶ ▲ Gardeners are discovering the joy of watching early morning ferns unfurl. Ornamental grasses are also popular.

FERNS AND ORNAMENTAL GRASSES

In the early morning as the birds sing, ferns unfurl and ornamental grasses shed their dewy bath. What better time is there to take a walk around the garden and watch the plants wake up. Ferns and ornamental grasses are enjoying a period of discovery by the gardener. You will enjoy exploring their distinctive colors and shapes.

Ferns

Osmunda regalis	zone 2	Royal fern
Onoclea sensibilis	zone 3	Sensitive fern
Matteuccia struthiopteris pensylvanica	zone 2	Ostrich fern
Adiantum pedatum	zone 3	Maidenhead fern

Ornamental Grasses

Briza media	zones 4–8	Quaking grass
Festuca ovina 'Glauca'	zones 4–9	Blue fescue
Miscanthus sinensis 'Gracillimus'	zone 4	Maiden grass

RASPBERRY MUFFINS WITH SWEET MINT BUTTER

1³/4 cups sifted all-purpose flour

³/4 teaspoon salt

¹/4 cup sugar

2 teaspoons double-acting baking powder

2 eggs

4 tablespoons melted butter

³/4 cup light cream

¹/4 cup raspberry jam

2 cups fresh raspberries

The Butter

¹/2 cup (1 stick) butter, softened to room temperature

3 tablespoons very finely minced mint leaves

2 tablespoons powdered confectioners' sugar

1 teaspoon fresh-squeezed lemon juice

Preheat oven to 400 degrees F. In a large mixing bowl, sift together sifted flour, salt, sugar, and baking powder. In a separate bowl, beat the eggs. Add to the eggs the melted butter, cream, and raspberry jam. Combine the liquid with the dry ingredients. Blend with a few swift strokes.

Gently fold in raspberries. Fill well-greased muffin tins two-thirds full. Bake 20 to 25 minutes, or until toothpick inserted in center of muffin comes out clean. Serve warm with fresh mint butter.

To make the butter, combine the butter, mint leaves, powdered sugar, and lemon juice in a small mixing bowl. Allow the butter to sit at room temperature for about 30 minutes to develop the flavors.

VEAL SAUSAGE EN CROÛTE WITH PEACH SYRUP

6 veal sausages (about 3 pounds)

One 1-pound package frozen puff pastry dough

1 egg white, beaten

The Syrup

1 cup sugar

¹/2 cup water

¹/2 cup peach schnapps

¹/4 teaspoon salt

2-inch piece stick cinnamon

2 whole cloves

5 ripe peaches, peeled, pitted and puréed

Preheat oven to 400 degrees F. Cut the puff pastry sheet into six strips cut the short way, about 2¹/2 inches wide. Roll one sausage in each puff pastry strip and brush with a little beaten egg white to seal the ends. Place end side down on cookie sheet and bake 10 to 15 minutes, or until pastry is brown and sausage cooked.

To make the syrup, combine sugar, water, schnapps, salt, cinnamon, and cloves in a medium-size saucepan over high heat. Bring to boil. Reduce heat to medium, and simmer 5 to 10 minutes, until syrup is slightly thickened. Remove cinnamon and cloves. Allow to cool slightly. Stir in peach purée. Serve with veal sausages. Makes 3 cups syrup.

© Steven Mark Needham/Envision

AUG

Beatrix Potter Birthday Party
for Twelve

Crudités with Sweet Satay Dipping Sauce
Peppered Cheese Straws
Classic Fried Chicken with Herbs
Confetti Coleslaw
Carrot Cake with Orange Frosting

There's a rule out there somewhere that says it is wise never to invite a greater number of guests than the age of the host or hostess. If you followed that thinking for this party, a two-year-old host would be very lonely and not have much fun.

The most important element in a children's party is grown-ups to see that the kids stay safe and happy. The most unnecessary element in a children's party is grown-ups. In other words, have them around but unseen, hovering like secret agents.

As you plan this party, turn yourself into a child and try to recall what details once charmed you at parties. Children love to eat with their hands, though their parents do not always like it. This menu is designed to be finger lickin' good and the kids will have a great time.

Beatrix Potter, if you remember, was notably unsentimental about her creations. She was a wise and uncompromising artist who drew from real life and after much study. Researching her work is something you will enjoy, and perhaps you and your child should plan this party together over *Peter Rabbit* bedtime stories with a stuffed Peter looking on.

Place mats and napkins bearing the Potter characters would, of course, be perfect today. To amuse themselves while they eat, the little guests can use crayons to color the animal characters.

One thing we know for sure is that children love a treasure hunt, and they will enthusiastically join the one you plan. If you can devise a treasure map using Potter characters, all the better.

One major point about such a competition: Everyone must get a prize.

What a wonderful time to hire a magician, a clown, or the artists who make creatures out of long balloons. A grown-up in a bunny costume would be superb. Adults should be few and far between at children's parties—maybe disguised is even better.

Illustration by Beatrix Potter, © Frederick Warne & Co., 1902,1987

Perhaps more than any other classic in children's literature, *Peter Rabbit* celebrates the garden as playground.

CRUDITÉS WITH SWEET SATAY DIPPING SAUCE

3 carrots, cut into 2-inch strips
3 celery stalks, cut into 2-inch strips
2 cucumbers, peeled and cut into 2-inch strips

The Sauce:
½ cup dark soy sauce
2 cups smooth peanut butter
½ cup sugar
2 cups water
1 tablespoon sesame oil

Cut vegetables and refrigerate.

In a small saucepan, combine soy sauce, peanut butter, sugar, and water over medium-high heat. Allow mixture to simmer 5 minutes, stirring con-stantly. If sauce is still thin, continue to simmer until thickened. Remove from heat; cool to room temperature. If sauce solidifies upon cooling, thin with a little hot water. Stir in sesame oil.

Arrange vegetables decoratively around a platter. Place sauce in a small bowl in the center.

PEPPERED CHEESE STRAWS

6 tablespoons (¾ stick) unsalted butter, at room temperature
¾ cup grated Parmesan cheese
3 tablespoons freshly ground black pepper
1 cup all-purpose flour
Paprika

Preheat oven to 350 degrees F. In a medium bowl, cream butter until fluffy. Beat in cheese and pepper. Blend in flour.

Divide dough into thirds; wrap each portion in plastic wrap and refrigerate until dough is firm, about 1 hour.

Roll out one portion of dough at a time, keeping remaining dough refriger-ated. To roll out dough, dust two sheets of plastic wrap with flour. Roll out dough between sheets of plastic wrap to approximately ⅛-inch thickness. Peel off top sheet of plastic. Cut rolled-out dough in 4 x ½-inch strips. Hold each strip at both ends. Twist in opposite directions so each strip has two twists. Arrange twists on ungreased baking sheets. Bake 10 minutes, or until golden brown. Remove from oven and sprinkle with paprika.

You will have no problem getting the children to eat their vegetables when you serve them with peanut buttery dipping sauce.

GARDEN LISTS FOR CHILDREN

Garden Friends	Garden Enemies
Praying mantis	Snail
Butterfly	Japanese beetle
Bee	Squash bug
Ladybug	Caterpillar
Earthworm	Aphid

Plants from Peter Rabbit's Garden

If you have children, they may enjoy growing a garden like the one in *Peter Rabbit*. Here are the vegetables mentioned in the book. Just like Peter Rabbit, you may find your young gardeners snitching from the garden.

Cucurbita pepo	annual	Pumpkin
Lactuca sativa	annual	Lettuce
Pisum sativum	annual	Pea
Zea mays everta	annual	Popcorn
Raphanus sativus	annual	Radish
Fragaria vesca	zone 5–6	Strawberry
Helianthus annuus	annual	Sunflower

CLASSIC FRIED CHICKEN WITH HERBS

5 cups vegetable oil

4 large eggs

³/₄ cup buttermilk

¹/₂ cup fresh-squeezed lemon juice

2 teaspoons salt

2 teaspoons freshly ground black pepper

3 tablespoons dried thyme

3 tablespoons dried oregano

3 cups seasoned dry bread crumbs

3 chickens, about 3 pounds each, cut into 10 pieces

In a 12-inch skillet over medium-high heat, or in electric frying pan, heat 4 cups oil to 375 degrees F, or until a 1-inch cube white bread turns brown in 60 seconds.

While oil heats, combine eggs, buttermilk, lemon juice, salt, pepper, thyme, and oregano in medium-size bowl; using wire whisk or fork, beat until smooth and well blended.

Place bread crumbs in 1-gallon resealable plastic bag. Working with 2 to 3 pieces of chicken at a time, dip first into egg mixture, letting excess drip back into bowl, shake in bag with crumbs to coat completely.

Carefully add enough chicken pieces

© Dick Luna/FPG International

to hot oil to fit in one layer without crowding. Cook, covered, 5 to 6 minutes on each side, until cooked through. Using tongs, transfer cooked chicken to cookie sheet lined with paper towels; if planning to serve hot, keep warm in oven set on lowest setting.

Add more oil if necessary. Allow temperature of oil to return to 375 degrees F before frying remaining chicken. Serve hot or at room temperature.

CONFETTI COLESLAW

1/2 cup mayonnaise

1/2 cup dairy sour cream

1/4 cup finely chopped fresh dill

1 tablespoon fresh-squeezed lemon juice

1/2 teaspoon freshly ground black pepper (optional)

1/2 teaspoon salt

2 teaspoons sugar

1 small head green cabbage, cored and finely shredded (about 6 cups)

1 red bell pepper, cored and diced

1 green bell pepper, cored and diced

4 large carrots, trimmed, peeled, and coarsely grated

In large bowl, combine mayonnaise, sour cream, dill, lemon juice, black pepper, salt, and sugar; stir to blend well.

Stir in cabbage, red and green bell peppers, and carrots. Stir to coat thoroughly. Refrigerate at least 1 hour or up to 24 hours. Serve chilled.

FUN THINGS IN THE GARDEN

Children will be especially intrigued by the garden if you make the following comparisons. You could make this into a game by asking them to match the animal or insect to the description.

The Acrobat	Common tree frog
The Dweller in a Stone House	Garden Snail
The Washer	Raccoon
The Silent Partner	Earthworm
The Animated Lanterns	Fireflies
The Night Fliers	Moths
The Spring Heralds	Robins and other songbirds
The Engineer	Spiders
The Friendly Enemy	Skunk
The Serenader	Cricket
The Demon of the Night	Bat
Dweller in Darkness	Mole
The Tree Tapper	Woodpecker
The Aerialist	Dragonfly
The Cacher	Squirrel
The Lazy Animal	Woodchuck
The Living Fossil	Possum

Illustration by Beatrix Potter, © Frederick Warne & Co., 1902, 1987

Your little guests will join Peter Rabbit in the garden, merry in his naughty antics.

SEPT

Intimate Dinner
for Four

*Goat Cheese Salad with Basil Vinaigrette
and Fresh Figs*

*Grilled or Broiled Red Snapper with Fresh
Mint and Garlic Marinade*

Julienned Cucumber Sauté

Lemon Thyme Pilaf

Chocolate Gateau with Espresso Buttercream

The mood is elegant, but not necessarily formal. A casual sophistication is called for. This might be a dinner between four good friends, or two couples, or it might be a way of introducing two single people.

Four is a pleasingly round number, so this night should just roll along without a hitch. The guest list is tiny, but there *are* guests, nonetheless, which means people to delight with your efforts—which is what entertaining is all about.

What a wonderful time to show off your garden, since taking a stroll around the garden does not mean taking yourself away from other guests. Instead, take them all with you, drinks in hand. The garden will be in fine shape, of course, since small-party planning has left you so much free time to prune and deadhead. You might want to plant some night-blooms if you have none; they will be lingeringly appreciated this leisurely evening.

"Intimate" means a time to let your hair down, a time to relax, a time to be with your friends. Tonight this is your party, too. Small as it is, you might consider getting some help so that you will not miss a story, a smile, or a compliment during the food preparation, the serving, and the clearing away.

Blooms from your garden floating in a low glass bowl would

make a wonderful centerpiece, complementing the low lights, the well-chosen china, the small vase and candle set at each place, the lacy napkins, the light laughter.

If the occasion celebrates an engagement, a beautifully wrapped gift for the couple—perhaps amusing instructions for married life—would be remembered always. If the guests are from far away, do not think a photo of you, your family, and your garden is too self-serving. On the contrary, it is respectful of your friendship, irreplaceable, and will always remind them of your intimate evening together.

If the toast of the evening is to a new job, a fine writing instrument would be a distinguished gift with which to send a guest to his or her new post. If the occasion is a blind date set up by you and your co-host, only one gift will do: exquisite care with the music. Any lapse into serious love songs will leave them wishing they had stayed home alone and sent out for pizza. All you have to do is keep the evening rolling along smoothly.

GOAT CHEESE SALAD WITH BASIL VINAIGRETTE AND FRESH FIGS

The Salad
1/2 head romaine lettuce
1/2 head radicchio
1 head bibb lettuce
1 cucumber, thinly sliced

The Dressing
1 large clove garlic
1/4 cup chopped fresh basil or 2 teaspoons dried
2 teaspoons Dijon-style mustard
2 tablespoons white wine
2 tablespoons champagne vinegar
1/4 cup extra virgin olive oil

The Cheese
1/2 cup fresh bread crumbs
1 large clove garlic, minced
1 tablespoon chopped fresh parsley
1 teaspoon salt
2 teaspoons freshly ground black pepper
One 8-ounce Montrachet goat cheese, sliced into four 1/2-inch rounds
1 egg, beaten
4 tablespoons olive oil
1 tablespoon unsalted butter
4 fresh figs, quartered

Trim, wash, and tear lettuces into bite-size pieces. Combine in large bowl. Add cucumber slices. Reserve.

To make the dressing, combine garlic, basil, mustard, wine, and vinegar in bowl of food processor or blender. With processor running, slowly drizzle olive oil in a thin stream until well blended. Reserve.

In a small bowl, combine bread crumbs, garlic, parsley, salt, and pepper. Mix well. Dip cheese into beaten egg, then coat in bread crumb mixture. Place on small platter and refrigerate until ready to use.

Preheat oven to lowest setting. In a 10-inch skillet over high heat, combine oil and butter. When hot, add goat cheese. Cook 2 to 3 minutes on each side, or until golden brown. Transfer to tray and keep warm in oven.

To serve, toss salad with dressing. Mound small amount of salad in center of each plate. Add one slice goat cheese and flank with fresh fig quarters.

GRILLED OR BROILED RED SNAPPER WITH FRESH MINT AND GARLIC MARINADE

1 large clove garlic
1/4 cup white wine vinegar
1/2 cup fresh mint leaves
1/2 cup extra virgin olive oil
1/2 teaspoon kosher salt
1 teaspoon sugar
Two 1-pound whole red snappers, filleted with skin

In the bowl of a food processor or blender, combine garlic, vinegar, mint, oil, salt, and sugar. Process until well blended and all mint leaves are finely chopped. Place red snapper in a shallow glass or ceramic dish so that they are in one layer. Pour marinade over fish and turn the pieces to coat well. Cover with plastic wrap and refrigerate for 30 minutes. Prepare grill or preheat broiler. Grill or broil 7 to 10 minutes on each side, or until fish is cooked through. Serve snapper with extra marinade, if desired.

JULIENNED CUCUMBER SAUTÉ

1 tablespoon butter

1 tablespoon extra virgin olive oil

3 small cucumbers, peeled, cut into 2-inch long julienne strips

¼ teaspoon salt

¼ teaspoon freshly ground white pepper

1 tablespoon finely chopped fresh coriander or 2 tablespoons coriander flowers

In a medium-size skillet over high heat, heat butter and oil. When butter has melted and oil is hot, about 1 minute, add cucumber. Cook, stirring constantly, 3 to 5 minutes, or until cooked through but still al dente. Remove from heat. Season with salt, pepper, and fresh coriander.

© Beverly G. Bowe

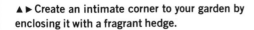
▲ ▶ **Create an intimate corner to your garden by enclosing it with a fragrant hedge.**

HEDGES

For occasions such as this, consider enclosing a part of your garden with hedges to create an outdoor "room."

To encourage your hedge to grow vigorously through the summer, trim one half of the new growth in early spring. Prune so your hedge is slightly broader at the bottom and narrower at the top.

Hedges 1 to 4 feet (32 cm to 120 cm) high

Berberis thunbergii	zone 4	Japanese barberry
Forsythia x 'Arnold Dwarf'	zone 5	Forsythia
Ribes alpinum	zone 2	Alpine currant

Hedges 4 to 10 feet (120 cm to 320 cm) high

Thuja occidentalis	zone 2	Arborvitae
Ilex glabra	zone 3	Inkholly
Euonymus alata	zone 3	Winged euonymus

Hedges 8 to 15 feet (250 cm to 480 cm) high

Ligustrum amurense	zone 3	Privet hedge
Tsuga sieboldii	zone 5	Siebold hemlock
Acer campestre	zone 4	Hedge maple

SEPT

With your garden thick and green, it is time to gild the lily. This day calls for more filling foods, such as a thick and hearty vegetable soup, potato salad, and a heavier wine, perhaps a Zinfandel. But the end of the growing season is, of course, still summer, and iced tea—perhaps sun-cured and seasoned with your own homegrown mint, of course—and iced coffee will still be on the menu.

The stars of your garden will not be seen as much as tasted and savored today, so you will need to supplement the garden area with pots of annuals. The later garden looks to you for its color, and in return it will contribute its finest green. Consider a wonderful Italian touch: a pot wrapped in a gaily colored scarf. Or if there is an area no longer blooming, why not bury an entire pot of blooms, for a faux flourish?

Now is the time for floral tablecloths: blue and white with cornflowers, smart crisp cotton with tiny rosebuds, perhaps matching the scarf wrapping a neighboring pot.

Your china is, perhaps, white, offsetting the vines and woody stems you have arranged on the table. For a centerpiece, what could be lovelier than a bowl of refreshing red or white grapes and fresh plump figs, promise of things to come?

In this often hot season, table placement is of prime

importance. You will want to take advantage of every breeze and bit of tree shade.

Today's music: memorytime, your own past played back gently as the season slips away. This is the last stretch of summertime, and new lives will soon begin. There is nostalgia about, as well as sweet celebration.

© Michael Grand

SALADE DE POMMES DE TERRE

2¹/₂ pounds all-purpose potatoes, peeled, cut into ¹/₂-inch dice

2 cups cooked fresh or frozen peas

¹/₃ cup chopped fresh mint

¹/₂ cup chopped fresh parsley

¹/₂ pound Norwegian smoked salmon, thinly sliced, cut into julienne strips

1 tablespoon Dijon-style mustard

¹/₄ cup balsamic vinegar

¹/₂ cup extra virgin olive oil

Salt and pepper, to taste

Romaine lettuce

12 slices bacon, cooked and cut into julienne strips

In a 3-quart saucepot, combine cubed potatoes with enough cold, salted water to cover. Bring to boil over high heat and cook until potatoes are just tender, about 15 to 20 minutes. Drain in colander. Allow to cool completely. Set aside. Do not run cold water over them to cool them as this will make them soggy.

Meanwhile, in a large mixing bowl, combine peas, mint, parsley, and salmon. Toss to blend thoroughly. Reserve.

To make dressing, combine mustard and vinegar in the bowl of a food processor. With processor still running, drizzle in olive oil until well blended. Season with salt and pepper to taste.

Combine cooled potatoes with smoked salmon mixture. Toss well. Add dressing and continue to toss to coat well. Serve over romaine lettuce leaves. Sprinkle with cooked bacon. Serve immediately.

© Jen Fong

Hearty wine and foods that reflect the abundance of the garden's harvest are called for this early evening, as two take time out to toast each other in the still-warm, open air.

VEAL CHOPS STUFFED WITH SPINACH, BASIL, AND SUNDRIED TOMATOES

10 veal chops, about 8-10 ounces each

Salt and pepper

2 tablespoons unsalted butter

2 tablespoons plus ¼ cup extra virgin olive oil

1 medium onion, finely chopped

3 large cloves garlic, crushed

10-ounce package frozen chopped spinach, thawed and drained thoroughly

½ cup sundried tomatoes in olive oil, thinly sliced

1 cup fresh white bread crumbs

½ cup chopped fresh basil or 2 tablespoons dried

Salt and pepper, to taste

The Sauce

¼ cup fresh-squeezed lemon juice

½ cup extra virgin olive oil

1 teaspoon salt

Chopped parsley

Preheat oven to 350 degrees F. Make a horizontal incision in the veal chops so as to create a pocket for the filling. Season both sides with salt and pepper.

Meanwhile, in a 10-inch skillet over medium-high heat, melt the butter with the olive oil. When hot, add the onion and the garlic. Cook, stirring constantly, 1 to 2 minutes, or until the onion is translucent. Add the spinach and cook, stirring, 1 to 2 minutes, until heated through. Add the sundried tomatoes and cook 2 minutes longer. Remove from heat. Stir in bread crumbs, basil, salt, and pepper. Reserve and let cool.

When filling is completely cooled, divide evenly among all the veal chops and stuff a generous amount into the pockets. Seal by simply pressing the two sides of the pocket together or secure with a metal skewer.

In a 12-inch skillet over high heat, add ¼ cup olive oil. When hot, add the veal in one layer. If necessary, cook the veal in two batches. Cook until lightly browned, about 1 to 2 minutes on each side. Transfer to shallow roasting pan and place in oven. Continue cooking about 10 to 15 minutes.

Meanwhile, in the same skillet used to sauté the veal chops, add lemon juice. Scrape particles off the bottom of the pan. Add the olive oil and cook until heated through. Add salt. Remove from heat. Spoon over veal chops and sprinkle with fresh parsley.

© Bill Margerin/FPG International

SEPT

Romantic Dinner
for Two

*Bitter Greens with Warm Bacon and Hot
Mustard Vinaigrette*

*Lobster and Sole Mousse with Vanilla
Buttersauce and Julienned Vegetables*

Coeurs à la Crème

It is a night for the language of flowers, for the unspoken to be revealed in scent and in song. Tall, pale pink or yellow candles will lend a soft, warm glow to your intimate table. They should harmonize comfortably with the centerpiece, which should be low and unobtrusive, with a subtle scent.

What songs do you love listening to together? Tape them. Make an effort to arrange the music system so that it is not overbearing. Nat King Cole and Nelson Riddle, Billie Holliday and Linda Ronstadt or the piano music of George Winston offer romantic tunes to create the mood for you beautifully.

You might prepare for this dinner by collecting photographs or memorabilia of shared memories and arranging them in an attractive book. These you can share for the first time over after-dinner drinks.

A dinner such as this is also a grand way to say, "We're going to have a baby," or "Why *don't* we have a baby?" It is a thoughtful way to start or end a vacation or a job, to celebrate a new house, a promotion, or the arrival home of a traveling partner.

Perhaps best of all, this might be a surprise dinner with a tender message: "I love you and I never forget it." If you are still dating, take this opportunity to introduce him or her to your tastes in food, coffee, laughs, gardens, and whatever else is important to you. What a wonderful way to break the ice. For this night, be sure your garden is perfectly lit, so that a stroll through it is irresistible, and your guest can see what you mean when you say, "My garden is my haven."

BITTER GREENS WITH WARM BACON AND HOT MUSTARD VINAIGRETTE

2 ounces sliced bacon, cut into ¹/₄-inch pieces

¹/₂ cup arugula, washed and stemmed

¹/₂ cup chicory, washed, cut into 1-inch pieces

¹/₂ cup escarole, washed, cut into 1-inch pieces

¹/₂ endive, sliced into 1-inch pieces

The Dressing:

2 tablespoons Chardonnay white wine vinegar

2 tablespoons hot mustard

Salt and freshly ground black pepper, to taste

In a small skillet over high heat, cook bacon 3 to 5 minutes, until crisp and golden brown. Remove bacon to paper towels to drain. Reserve.

Remove pan from heat. Drain all but 4 tablespoons bacon grease from pan. Add vinegar and whisk in mustard until well blended. Season with salt and black pepper to taste.

Toss greens. Before dressing salad, warm vinaigrette over low heat 1 to 2 minutes. Add bacon. Pour dressing over salad and toss well.

LOBSTER AND SOLE MOUSSE WITH VANILLA BUTTERSAUCE AND JULIENNED VEGETABLES

³/₄ pound fillet of sole, cut into 1-inch pieces

2 large eggs

¹/₄ teaspoon salt

¹/₂ teaspoon white pepper

¹/₄ teaspoon cayenne pepper

²/₃ cup heavy cream

1 to 1¹/₂ pounds cooked lobster, tail and claw meat removed and cut into small chunks

The Vanilla Buttersauce

¹/₂ cup fish stock

¹/₂ cup Reisling wine vinegar

4 large shallots, finely minced

1 clove garlic, minced

¹/₂ teaspoon whole black peppercorns

1 vanilla bean, split lengthwise

¹/₂ cup (1 stick) unsalted butter

Salt and white pepper, to taste

¹/₄ cup chopped chives

The Vegetables

2 carrots, pared and julienned

1 small zucchini, julienned

1 tablespoon olive oil

1 tablespoon chopped chives

Preheat oven to 375 degrees F. In a bowl of a food processor, process the

© Wolfgang Kaehle

For a romantic evening such as this, a pre-dinner walk, hand-in-hand, down a twilight path to a secret garden is an irresistible delight.

sole until coarsely chopped. Add eggs, salt, and peppers. Process until smooth. With processor still running, slowly add cream in a thin stream until well blended. Scrape fish mousse into large mixing bowl. Fold in lobster meat with a spatula until evenly distributed.

Grease two 3- x 2-inch-deep molds with butter. Place in a deep ovenproof baking dish large enough to hold both molds. Fill the molds with the fish mousse. Tap the bottoms of the fish molds firmly to remove any air bubbles. Smooth the molds with a knife so the mousse is flush with the side of the molds. With the molds in the baking dish, fill the dish with enough hot water to come within ¹/₄ inch of the tops of the molds. Place on top of the stove over high heat. Bring to boil. Cover the molds with a piece of wax paper so that it rests directly on top of the mousse. Place in the oven and bake 25 to 30 minutes, or until a toothpick inserted in the middle comes out clean. Remove from oven and allow mousse to sit 5 minutes before unmolding.

To make the sauce, combine fish stock, vinegar, shallots, garlic, peppercorns, and vanilla bean in a two-quart saucepan over high heat. Bring to boil and allow it to reduce until almost dry. Reduce heat to medium. Add butter all at once and whisk until completely melted. Strain through a fine-meshed sieve into a small bowl. Season with salt and pepper and chopped chives.

Sauté ½ cup *each* julienned carrots and zucchini in olive oil until crisp-tender. Place Vanilla Buttersauce on the bottom of each plate. Make a small mound of vegetables at the head of the plate and unmold the mousse to rest directly underneath it. Garnish with fresh whole chives or more sauce, if desired.

THE SECRET GARDEN

"It's a secret garden, and I'm the only one in the world who wants it to be alive."
Frances Hodgson Burnett
The Secret Garden

Make a part of your garden into your own special place, but one which you share with your friends. You may want to conceal a section of the yard with a hedge, then plant it with your favorite plants and flowers. Here is a list of some of the plants in *The Secret Garden*. Let them inspire you.

Hedera helix	zone 5	Untrimmed English ivy
Malus sargentii	zone 4	Dwarf apple tree
Syringa vulgaris	zone 3	Lilac
Prunus domestica 'Artic'	zone 3	Plum tree
Prunus avium		Sweet cherry tree
Rhododendron arborescens	zone 4	Rhododendron

Spring Flowers

Crocus korolkowii	zone 6	Crocus
Galanthus nivalis	zone 3	Snowdrop
Narcissus poeticus	zone 4	Yellow daffodil
Delphinium tricorne	zone 5	Larkspur
Primula vulgaris	zone 5	Primrose
Aquilegia x hybrida	zone 4	Columbine
Antirrhinum majus	annual	Snapdragon

Summer Flowers

Iris kaempferi	zone 4	Iris
Lilium candidum	zone 4	White lily
Delphinium grandiflora	zone 2–3	White and blue delphinium
Campanula americana	annual	Campanula
Papaver nudicaule	zone 2	Poppy
Climbing rose Constance Spry		Climbing rose

NOV

Beaujolais is the light, fragrant, delicious *vin du pays* of southern Burgundy, the country just northwest of Lyon. From a small, compact area of vine-covered hills, it is one of the most popular and best-loved wines of France. It is fruity and full-bodied with a special, almost spicy flavor, an eminently drinkable red table wine that must be served at the temperature of the cellar rather than that of the dining room. Beaujolais must be drunk young—the younger the better according to many gourmets—for it is fragile. Light chilling softens the edges of its youthful charm and heightens its flavor. Nouveaus are so light-hearted that American vint-

ners who make them say they are not only fun to drink, but a pleasure to make.

"Vendage!" is joyfully shouted by the harvestors as the French gamay grapes are carefully harvested in October. This is a boisterous occasion, and, lest there be any doubt about the reason for the celebration, grapevines encircle the steaming casseroles in the center of the table set up after the harvest for the families and friends who brought in the bounty.

You might carry on the spirit of *vendage* by presenting your guests with colorful bowls overflowing with grapes or erecting a temporary latticework arbor on which to display grapevines or the closest you can come to them—English ivy, perhaps. Some Portuguese bowls are actually shaped like grapes and would convey the mood splendidly. This is the time for bright purple tablecloths and green napkins, for anything leafy and bountiful.

This is a happy wine-tasting, without any pretensions. No one has tasted this *Beaujolais Nouveau* before, so everyone bcomes an expert. The food that accompanies the new arrival should be as French and special as the wine. Venison with Sauce Poivrade, pâté, and an assortment of cheeses will all highlight the distinctive flavor of the wine.

Anything French is welcome here, in fact. The gift that would be most cherished as the guests reluctantly leave your harvest garden would be a bottle for each to take home, a purple ribbon round its neck, perched in a charming rattan wine holder. Each ribbon might be tagged with the guest's name in French!

▲ ▶ This delicious meal is complemented by a fresh pear tart.

PARMESAN-BAKED FENNEL

6 to 8 small fennel bulbs

2 tablespoons unsalted butter

One 13³/4-ounce can low-sodium chicken broth

¹/2 teaspoon freshly ground black pepper

¹/2 cup grated Parmesan cheese

Preheat oven to 400 degrees F. Cut the tops of the fennel bulbs, trim base, and pull off any tough outer leaves. Cut in half. Cook the fennel in enough boiling, salted water to cover. Simmer for about 15 minutes, or until just tender. Drain the fennel and arrange cut side down in a baking dish. Dot with butter; add broth and pepper and sprinkle with Parmesan cheese. Bake about 30 minutes.

VENISON STEAKS WITH SAUCE POIVRADE

1 cup dry red wine

¹/4 cup red wine vinegar

7 whole cloves, crushed

1 tablespoon black peppercorns, crushed

2 tablespoons juniper berries

2 teaspoons salt

2 tablespoons chopped fresh thyme or 2 teaspoons dried

2 cups olive oil plus 2 teaspoons olive oil

Eight to ten 8-ounce venison steaks, about ¹/2 to 1 inch thick

1 tablespoon butter

The Sauce Poivrade

2 tablespoons vegetable oil

1 carrot, pared and chopped

1 medium onion, chopped

3 sprigs parsley

1 bay leaf

¼ cup all-purpose flour

3 cups beef broth

½ cup marinade

10 peppercorns

½ cup dry red wine

Salt to taste

1½ tablespoons freshly ground black pepper

In a large ceramic or glass bowl, combine wine, vinegar, cloves, peppercorns, berries, salt, thyme, and 2 cups oil. Add venison steaks and marinate 8 hours, or overnight. Remove from marinade. Reserve marinade for sauce.

To make the sauce, heat 2 table-spoons vegetable oil in a 12-inch skillet over high heat. When hot, sauté carrot and onion until tender, about 3 to 5 minutes. Add parsley and bay leaf. Sprinkle with flour. Cook, stirring, 3 to 5 minutes. Add beef broth and ¼ cup marinade used for venison steaks. Bring to boil, reduce heat to low and simmer 1 hour. Add peppercorns and simmer an additional 5 minutes.

Strain sauce through a fine-meshed sieve, return to heat and add remaining ¼ cup marinade. Cook slowly 30 minutes longer and then add red wine. Season with salt to taste and finely ground black pepper to make a spicy sauce. Transfer sauce to serving dish and keep warm while cooking venison.

In a 12-inch skillet, heat remaining 2 teaspoons olive oil and 1 tablespoon butter over high heat. When hot, add venison. Cook 3 to 5 minutes on each side, depending on desired doneness.

The vendage is France's celebration of the bounty and beauty of the grape. Homage to the sun, rain, and rich earth that nurtures the fruit, your vendage will call for overflowing displays of the grapes themselves and for hardy plates and glasses that will capture the color and excitement of the crisp new wine's first pouring.

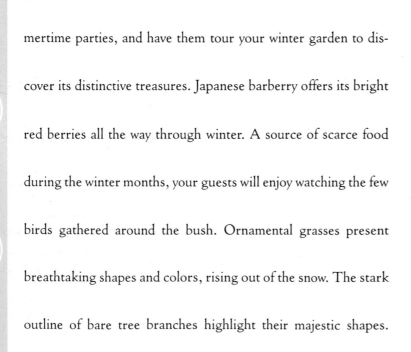

Winter Twilight Party
for Twenty

*Hot Mulled Cider

*Blue Cheese Spread

*Turkey and Spinach Phyllo Rolls

Sweet Potato and Carrot Purée

Brussels Sprouts with Chestnuts

Fig Pudding with Hard Sauce

The weather has turned cold and your garden is snow-covered, but it is still beautiful in its dormant state. Or is it really dormant? Invite your friends who know your garden well from many summertime parties, and have them tour your winter garden to discover its distinctive treasures. Japanese barberry offers its bright red berries all the way through winter. A source of scarce food during the winter months, your guests will enjoy watching the few birds gathered around the bush. Ornamental grasses present breathtaking shapes and colors, rising out of the snow. The stark outline of bare tree branches highlight their majestic shapes.

Take pictures, then bring them out at a summer party when the garden is full and lush. You'll be able to see the way the branches and bushes, bursting with life, are engineered for their summer beauty.

Do not be daunted by the early dusk of winter. Celebrate the twilight, a bewitching hour, and begin your party as the night starts to fall. Take your guests for a tour right away, so they can watch the garden change and move with the setting sun. Later, turn on the lights and invite them to reacquaint themselves with the night winter garden, another place altogether. Spotlights shooting up into bare, snow-coated branches are dramatic and eerie. A berry-covered bush lighted from behind could be the proverbial burning bush.

If your party is held around the holidays, or if you just feel like it, ask your guests to help you decorate your garden to go with the season. String popcorn and cranberries, then hang them from the trees for the birds to share in your winter feast. Rope evergreen over the banisters, deck railings, and fence. Another festive touch is candles—in hands while touring the garden, on tables, in bags along the walkway. Set your table with scented candles—bayberry, for intance, to complement the lovely bush in your garden.

Your guests will need something to warm them when they return from their winter twilight walk. Mulled cider, both spiked and sober, will warm the hands, the body, and the soul. Serve traditional and heartwarming foods, delicacies of the season. Turkey and Spinach Phyllo Rolls are a handheld twist on the traditional entree, reminiscent of the pasties of Dickens' novels. The hardy flavor of blue cheese spread is complemented by the mellower sweet potato and carrot purée. Chestnuts are a perennial winter favorite; serve some with Brussels sprouts, but set some aside for roasting over an open fire. End your meal with comforting figgy pudding and rum- and nutmeg-laced hard sauce, just like mother always made.

Winter is the time when traditions are brought out and enjoyed, both because of the holidays that open the season and the need to warm the soul in a cold climate. This party, with its beautiful bare branches and noise-muffling snowy setting can be the beginnings of your own traditions. After the first year, your guests will be looking forward to the yearly twilight walk almost as much as they look forward to the first jonquils and tulips.

HOT MULLED CIDER

1 gallon cider
2 teaspoons whole cloves
4 whole cardamom pods
4 sticks cinnamon
1/4 cup fresh-squeezed lemon juice

Combine above ingredients in an 8-quart saucepot over medium-high heat. Heat well, for about 15 minutes, but do not boil. Keep warm over low heat.

BLUE CHEESE SPREAD

2 cups crumbled blue or Roquefort cheese
8 ounce package cream cheese, softened
1/4 cup cream sherry
1/4 cup dairy sour cream
1 tablespoon Worcestershire sauce
1/4 teaspoon cayenne pepper
2 tablespoons fresh-squeezed lemon juice

In the bowl of a food processor, combine the above ingredients. Process until smooth. Scrape cheese spread into serving dish or crock. Serve with assorted crackers or toast points.

TURKEY AND SPINACH PHYLLO ROLLS

2 tablespoons vegetable oil
1 small onion, finely chopped
3 large cloves garlic, crushed
1/2 pound ground turkey
1 teaspoon salt
1 1/2 teaspoons freshly ground black pepper
1/2 teaspoon hot red pepper flakes
10-ounce package frozen chopped spinach, thawed and drained
1 cup farmer cheese or pot cheese
1/2 pound phyllo pastry sheets
1/2 cup or more melted butter

Preheat oven to 450 degrees F. To an 8-inch skillet over high heat, add oil. When oil is hot, add onion. Cook, stirring, 3 to 5 minutes, until onion is

Many shrubs, such as scarlet firethorn, offer delightful colored berries to winter garden partygoers.

transparent. Add garlic and cook 30 seconds longer. Add turkey, breaking up with fork, and cook until meat is cooked through, about 5 to 8 minutes. Season with salt and black and red peppers.

Remove from heat. Stir in thawed, drained spinach and the cheese. Mix until well blended. Adjust seasonings if necessary. Let cool to room temperature.

Cut phyllo into strips about 4 inches wide and 6 inches long. Take one strip and brush with melted butter. Keep the remaining strips covered with plastic wrap at all times to prevent drying. Place about 2 teaspoons mixture at the end of pastry. Fold up once then fold in sides and roll up. Brush all the sides with butter and place on a cookie sheet. Repeat this procedure until all the filling is used.

Bake 15 minutes, or until the pastries are golden brown. Remove from oven. Allow to cool slightly. Serve warm.

© Steven Mark Needham/Envision

POMANDERS

Pomanders, fruit decorated with whole cloves and encrusted with fragrant spices, are a wonderful holiday or winter decoration. They are easy to make, even for children, and will scent your closets or drawers long after the holidays. Here are step-by-step instructions.

You will need the following fruits and spices:
An assortment of firm oranges, lemons, and apples
Several packages of whole cloves
Cinnamon, ground cloves, allspice, ground nutmeg, ground orris root
Several yards of ribbon

In a large bowl, mix together

4 parts cinnamon	1 part nutmeg
2 parts ground cloves	1 part orris root
1 part allspice	

Stick the whole cloves, by stem, into the fruits in a creative pattern or at random. Leave an even space, the width of your ribbon, around the center of the fruit.

Bury the pomanders in the spice mixture in a large bowl. Stir and turn the mixture about once a week, making sure you keep the pomanders buried. Keep the fruits buried for 6 weeks, until they are hardened.

When the fruits are hard, you will wrap the ribbon around them. Cut a piece of ribbon about 4 times the circumference of the fruit. Fold the ribbon in half, wrap it around the fruit, then pull the ribbon end through the loop at the end of the ribbon and pull it tight. Tie the loose ends of the ribbon in a bow, so you can hang the pomander.

Another alternative is a romantic rose pomander for Valentine's Day.
You will need:

Styrofoam balls	Glue
Ribbon	Rose oil or spray
Dried rose buds	

Pull a piece of ribbon through the ball with a needle and thread, or leave a space and attach the ribbon later as described for fruit pomanders.

Glue the rosebuds in a circular pattern around the ball until it is completely covered, except for the ribbon groove, if necessary.

Sprinkle the ball with rose oil or spray.

JAN

Bon Voyage Party
for Twelve

Thai-Style Shrimp and Papaya Salad
Supreme de Volaille aux Sesame
String Beans Julienne with Shiitake Mushrooms
Lemon Tart

A well-thought-out Bon Voyage Party can be a touching, long-remembered experience—a gathering of friends that strengthens long-distance connections and eases loneliness. Fortunate is the man, woman, or family who greets the moving van or the cruise ship after a party such as this, forever close to friends left behind.

If the party is celebrating a long-distance move and separation from friends and loved ones, the favors to be given will be heart-felt ones, and the most popular item on the menu will be memories. But this party can definitely make the move more fun.

If the honored guests are going to another region or another country for work-related reasons, or on sabbatical or holiday, the cuisine of the region or country of destination will determine the menu and the mood. The party menu presented here would be an appropriate send-off for any seagoing travelers, since the menu is international and continental, as on a cruise ship. A nice accompaniment to this fare would be a simple sparkling wine.

One recent successful going away party was given by a group of friends for a popular couple who were moving to Atlanta from New York. The hostess asked everyone to write a letter containing his or her favorite stories about or memories of the departing couple. These were mounted in a leather-bound book bought for the occasion. The loving thoughts were continued when it came time to toast the couple and the fifty guests offered verbal good wishes. All the foods served, in this case, spoke with a decided Southern accent. Such a party is a great occasion for inviting people of mixed ages, by the way, to enhance the rich family feeling.

The favorite foods of the honored guests would also be thoughtful menu choices, especially if there is no distinct, inspiring cuisine waiting for them at the end of the impending move. But if their cruise will wind up in the Caribbean, for instance, what a fun opportunity to help the vacationers get into the mood by giving them a taste of wildly colorful clothing, steel drums, and fancy fruits. If the move is to Santa Fe or Cape Cod, Sardinia or Provence, your menu choices will be as easily researched as your decorative and musical schemes.

If the honorees will be departing by ship, a colorful wooden boat into which gifts can be deposited would be a wonderful touch. If by air, why not an old-fashioned barnstormer bearing gifts?

No matter where your honored guests are going, by all means have on hand the two most universally joyful send-off symbols of all: free-flowing champagne and bright, happy streamers.

THAI-STYLE SHRIMP AND PAPAYA SALAD

2 pounds medium shrimp, peeled, deveined, and cooked

6 green onions, thinly sliced

4 tablespoons chopped fresh cilantro

4 teaspoons chopped fresh mint

4 large kirby pickling cucumbers, sliced lengthwise into 1/2-inch strips, then cut on the bias into 1/4-inch pieces

2 large red bell peppers, seeded, diced into 1/2-inch pieces

3 large ripe papayas, peeled, seeded, cut into 1/2-inch chunks

Two 3-inch pieces fresh gingerroot, peeled, cut into chunks

6 large cloves garlic

Juice from 2 limes

1/2 cup low-sodium soy sauce

1/2 cup rice wine vinegar

1 1/2 cups vegetable oil

2 to 4 teaspoons hot Chinese chili oil

16 cups assorted salad greens

In a large mixing bowl, combine cooled shrimp, onions, cilantro, mint, cucumbers, red pepper, and papayas. Toss well. Cover with plastic wrap and refrigerate.

Meanwhile, in the bowl of a food processor, combine ginger, garlic, lime juice, soy sauce, and rice wine vinegar. Blend until ginger and garlic are finely chopped. With processor still running, slowly add vegetable oil in a thin stream. Add chili oil.

Combine salad dressing with shrimp salad and toss thoroughly to blend well. Divide greens evenly among 12 large plates. Spoon equal amounts of the salad in the center of each plate.

© Balthazar Korab

SUPREME DE VOLAILLE AUX SESAMES

6 whole boneless, skinless chicken breasts, cut in half

Salt, to taste

Freshly ground black pepper, to taste

1 1/2 cups sesame seeds

3/4 cup (1 1/2 sticks) unsalted butter

Juice from 2 lemons

Place chicken breasts between two pieces of wax paper and pound lightly with a mallet. Sprinkle with salt and pepper. Dredge pieces on all sides in sesame seeds.

In a 12-inch skillet, heat 4 tablespoons butter over high heat. When hot, add chicken and cook 5 minutes on each side. Transfer to serving dish, and keep warm in oven. Heat the remaining butter and add the lemon juice. Swirl around until it is nutty brown. Pour over the chicken and serve.

SOURCES

Outdoor Audio Resources

Consultants/Acoustic Designers
H.W. Steinberg, Engineer
Linear Design
46 Ahnert Avenue
North Haledon, New Jersey 07508
(201) 423-1359

Resources
Atlas/Soundolier Loudspeaker Products
1859 Intertech Drive
Fenton, Missouri 63026

Bertagni Electroacoustic Systems
343 Fischer Street
Costa Mesa, California 92626

Bose Corporation
The Mountain
Framingham, Massachusetts 01701

Consolidated Electronic Wire and Cable
11044 King Street
Franklin Park, Illinois 60131

JWD
3215 Canton Street
P.O. Box 26177
Dallas, Texas 75266

Minneapolis Speaker Company
3806 Grand Avenue South
Minneapolis, Minnesota 55409

OWI Incorporated
1160 Mahalo Place
Compton, California 90220

Rockustics Incorporated
720-G Billings Street
Aurora, Colorado 80011

Sonic Systems, Incorporated
737 Canal Street
Bldg. 23B
Stamford, Connecticut 06902

TOA Designer Speakers
TOA Electric Company, Ltd.
Kobe, Japan

Waterworks Acoustics
3365 Fernside Boulevard
Alameda, California 94501

West Penn Wire Corporation
P.O. Box 762
2833 West Chestnut Street
Washington, Pennsylvania 15301

Outdoor Lighting Resources

Dover Design
Dept. G-3
2175 Beaver Valley Pike
New Providence, Pennsylvania 17560

Geisha Corporation
151 E. Sunset Road
Henderson, Nevada 89015

Genie House
P.O. Box 2478
Red Lion Road
Vincentown, New Jersey 08088

Hanover Lantern
470 High Street
Hanover, Pennsylvania 17331

Philip Hawk and Company
159 E. College Avenue
Pleasant Gap, Pennsylvania 16823

Hubbell Lighting Division
2000 Electric Way
Christiansburg, Virginia 24073

Intermatic, Incorporated
Intermatic Plaza
Spring Grove, Illinois 60081

Kyoto Design
409 East Street
Healdsburg, California 95448

Liteform Designs
Dept. G., P.O. Box 3316
Portland, Oregon 97208

Loran Lightscaping, Incorporated
1705 E. Colton
Redlands, California 92374

Sculptures By Schmidt, Incorporated
1320 N. Walnut
P.O. Box 116
Beloit, Kansas 67420

Thomas Industries, Incorporated
Residential Division
95 Breckenridge Lane
Ste. G50
Louisville, Kentucky 40207

Toro Company, Home Improvement Division
5300 Shoreline Boulevard
Mound, Minnesota 55364

The Washington Copper Works
South Street
Washington, Connecticut 06793

Garden Art

Asian Artifacts
P.O. Box 2494
Oceanside, California 92054

Clapper's
1125 Washington Street
West Newton, Massachusetts 02165

Florentine Craftsmen
46–24 28th Street
Long Island City, New York 11101

Gardener's Eden
P.O. Box 7303
San Francisco, California 94120

Hen Feathers & Company
10 Ballingomingo Road
Gulph Hills, Pennsylvania 19428

International Terra-Cotta, Incorporated
690 N. Robertson Boulevard
Los Angeles, California 90069

New England Garden Ornaments
38 E. Brookfield Road
North Brookfield, Massachusetts 01535

Smith & Hawken
25 Corte Madera
Mill Valley, California 94941

Southern Statuary & Stone
3401 Fifth Avenue South
Birmingham, Alabama 35222

United Outdoor Products
120 S. Raymond Avenue
Pasadena, California 91105

The Well-Furnished Garden
5635 West Boulevard
Vancouver, British Columbia V6M3W7

Wind & Weather
P.O. Box 2320
Mendocino, California 95460

Outdoor Furniture

Barlow Tyrie
65 Great Valley Parkway
Malvern, Pennsylvania 19355

Brandywine Garden Furniture
24 Phoenixville Pike
Malvern, Pennsylvania 19355

British-American Marketing Services, Ltd.
118 Pickering Way
Lionville, Pennsylvania 19353

Charleston Battery Bench, Incorporated
191 King Street
Charleston, South Carolina 29401

Cypress Street Center
Dept. H
350 Cypress Street
Fort Bragg, California 95437

Dunis Studios
Rte. 3, Box 3125
Bulverde, Texas 78163

Lister by Geebro
4600 Highlands Parkway, Ste. A
Smyrna, Georgia 30082

Lloyd/Flanders All-Weather Wicker
3010 10th Street
P.O. Box 500
Menominee, Michigan 49858

Lyon-Shaw, Incorporated
1538 Salisbury Boulevard
West Salisbury, North Carolina 28144

Mail Order Mall
P.O. Box 3006
Lakewood, New Jersey 08701

Moultrie Manufacturing Company
P.O. Drawer 1179
Moultrie, Georgia 31776

Palacek
P.O. Box 225
Sta. A
Richmond, California 94808

Sittin' Easy Classic Oak Furniture
P.O. Box 180
Eagle Springs, North Carolina 27242

Summit Furniture, Incorporated
P.O. Box S
Carmel, California 93921

Tropitone Furniture Company
P.O. Box 3197
Sarasota, Florida 33578
    or
5 Marconi
Irvine, California 92718

Wood Classics
Rte. 1, Box 455E
High Falls, New York 12440

Woodard
317 Elm Street
Owosso, Michigan 48867

Wood-Lot Farms
Star Route 1
Shady, New York 12479

Outdoor Serving Equipment

The Chef's Catalog
3215 Commercial Avenue
Northbrook, Illinois 60062

Joan Cook
3200 SE 14th Avenue
Fort Lauderdale, Florida 33316

C. R. Gibson
32 Knight Street
Norwalk, Connecticut 06856

Sue Fisher King
3067 Sacramento Street
San Francisco, California 94115

Gardening Sources

Bow House Incorporated
P.O. Box 228
Bolton, Massachusetts 01740

Paul Ecke Poinsettias
Box 488
Encinitas, California 92024

Ivywood Gazebo
Third Floor, P.O. Box 9
Fairview Village, Pennsylvania 19409

Kinsman Company
River Road
Point Pleasant, Pennsylvania 18950

The Mailorder Association of Nurseries
8683 Doves Fly Way
Laurel, Maryland 20707

Mrs. McGregor's Garden Shop
4801-H First Street North
Arlington, Virginia 22203

Petals
1 Aqueduct Road
White Plains, New York 10606

White Flower Farm Catalog
Litchfield, Connecticut 06759

Essential Catalogs for Outdoor Entertaining

Brookstone
15 Vose Farm Road
P.O. Box 806
Peterborough, New Hampshire 03460

Carillon
Rte. 2, Box 122
Banks, Oregon 97106

Colonial Garden Kitchens
P.O. Box 66
Hanover, Pennsylvania 17333

Crate and Barrel
P.O. Box 3057
Northbrook, Illinois 60065

Roberta Fortune's Almanac
150 Chestnut Street
San Francisco, California 94111

Gardener's Eden
P.O. Box 7307
San Francisco, California 94120

Gump's
250 Post Street
San Francisco, California 94108

Hammacher Schlemmer
9180 LeSaint Drive
Fairfield, Ohio 45014

Leichtung Workshops
4944 Commerce Parkway
Cleveland, Ohio 44128

Plow and Hearth
301 Madison Road
P.O. Box 830
Orange, Virginia 22960

Potpourri
Dept. 151
120 North Meadows Road
Medfield, Massachusetts 02052

Pottery Barn
P.O. Box 7044
San Francisco, California 94120

Rose & Gerard
55 Sunnyside
Mill Valley, California 94941

Smith & Hawken
25 Corte Madera
Mill Valley, California 94941

Solutions
P.O. Box 6878
Portland, Oregon 97228

Trifles
P.O. Box 620050
Dallas, Texas 75262

Lillian Vernon
510 South Fulton Avenue
Mount Vernon, New York 10550

Williams-Sonoma
P.O. Box 7456
San Francisco, California 94120

Wind & Weather
The Albion Street Water Tower
P.O. Box 2320
Mendocino, California 95460

Worldwide Games
Dept. 2117
Colchester, Connecticut 06415

LIQUID MEASURE EQUIVALENTS

3 teaspoons = 1 tablespoon
2 tablespoons = 1 fluid ounce
4 tablespoons = $\frac{1}{4}$ cup = 2 fluid ounces
5 tablespoons + 1 teaspoon = $\frac{1}{3}$ cup = $2\frac{2}{3}$ ounces
8 tablespoons = $\frac{1}{2}$ cup = 4 fluid ounces
10 tablespoons = $\frac{2}{3}$ cup
12 tablespoons = $\frac{3}{4}$ cup
16 tablespoons = 1 cup = 8 fluid ounces
2 cups = 16 fluid ounces = 1 pint
4 cups = 32 fluid ounces = 1 quart
8 cups = 64 fluid ounces = $\frac{1}{2}$ gallon
4 quarts = 128 fluid ounces = 1 gallon

METRIC CONVERSION TABLE

TO CHANGE	TO	MULTIPLY BY
teaspoons	milliliters	5
tablespoons	milliliters	15
fluid ounces	milliliters	30
ounces	grams	28
cups	liters	0.24
pints	liters	0.47
quarts	liters	0.95
gallons	liters	3.8
pounds	kilograms	0.45
Fahrenheit	Celsius	5/9 after subtracting 32

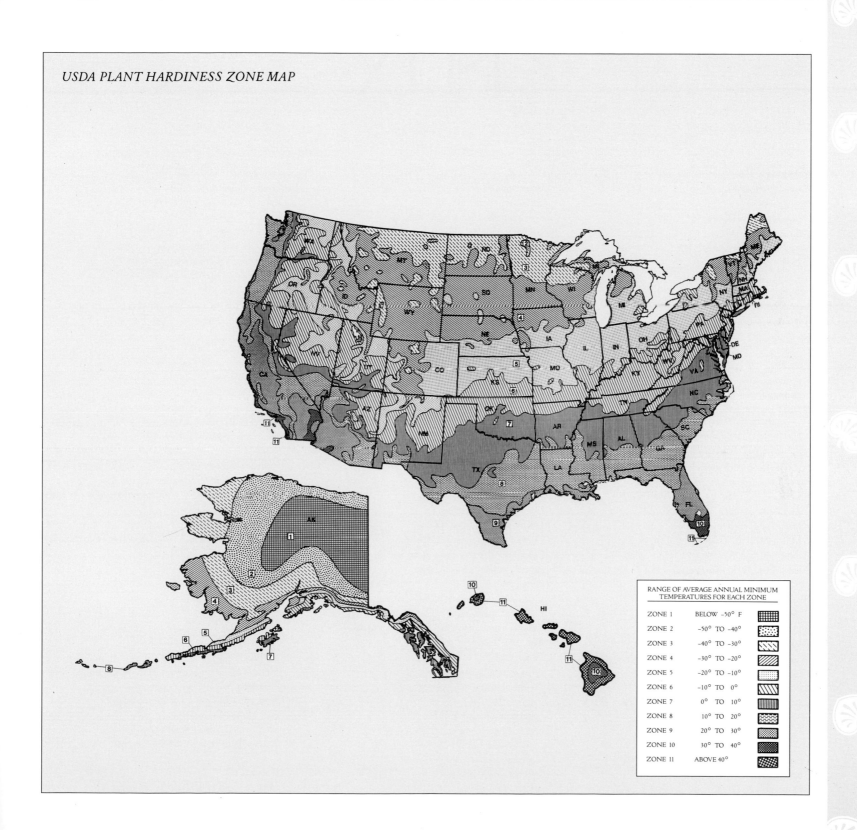

USDA PLANT HARDINESS ZONE MAP

RANGE OF AVERAGE ANNUAL MINIMUM TEMPERATURES FOR EACH ZONE		
ZONE 1	BELOW –50° F	
ZONE 2	–50° TO –40°	
ZONE 3	–40° TO –30°	
ZONE 4	–30° TO –20°	
ZONE 5	–20° TO –10°	
ZONE 6	–10° TO 0°	
ZONE 7	0° TO 10°	
ZONE 8	10° TO 20°	
ZONE 9	20° TO 30°	
ZONE 10	30° TO 40°	
ZONE 11	ABOVE 40°	

INDEX

ACKNOWLEDGEMENTS

Any woman who will stop still in the middle of a busy afternoon to cheerfully share her wisdom about Cole Porter, Beatrix Potter, and flea market pottery is a woman after our own hearts. Sharyn Grossman, our *sine qua non*, is a bright fire at the heart of this book. She lent both expertise and sheer delight to virtually every page and encouragement to every step. We raise our party glasses to her.

With the same heartfelt toast we hail the patient and wonderful Susan Davidson, and thank her for a charming, utterly essential New Haven day.

To Gill and Harry Patterson, Scott Markman and Toshi Kawahara, "cheers" for their inspired examples and their unabashed love for their land and their friends.

Cynthia Atwood, the first expert interviewed for this book, set the tone for candor and helpfulness; we thank her, as we do Gardner W. Hubbard and his very helpful staff, Pat King, Lisa Stamm Booher, Harvey Steinberg and Mark Gantt, Cheri Wagner, Nikol Hegarty, and Jon Imparato. To dear old friend Shirley Williams, prized writer for the Louisville, Kentucky, *Courier-Journal*, a special salute with the best bourbon money can buy for her expert assistance.

To landscape architect Dan Stewart, another old friend, many thanks for his guidance and support. And to Christina Lightfoot, a grateful embrace for hers.

To Elizabeth Sabo and her warm, welcoming Connecticut family, our love and gratitude.

A major thank you to Anson and Ellen Peckham, and deepest appreciation always.

Deirdre Colby, mother of this bright idea, matchmaker for book and author, imaginative resource for every theme and element, please accept our warmest thanks. And gratitude to the indefatigable Ann Price and to Karla Olson, an excellent editorial guide and a joy to work with.

To Elissa and Mary Napolin, to Jayne, to Victoria, and to the exquisite Starchild, gratitude from every dimension.

Thank you, Arline Moriarty, for absolutely everything.

Welcome, little Kia, to the world of friends and flowers.

And, finally, a toast to the radiant memory of Andrea Hardy Prentice, at home in our garden, smiling.